"Deftly and brilliantly, Rabbi David Zaslow shows us how the ancient biblical account of the Exodus from Egypt dances and echoes through the centuries as the paradigm of the quest for equality and independence for people of all faiths and communities. His cogent and compelling vision of our yearning as children of God who strive for equality, autonomy, and self-determination enflames our souls and gives hope to all humankind. Redemption! Liberation! Freedom! Then and Now!"

—RABBI WAYNE DOSICK, PhD, author of *Living Judaism* and
The Real Name of God

"Accessible, stimulating resource! Rabbi Zaslow offers fascinating literal, geographical, and metaphorical verse-by-verse sources and interpretation to power your spiritual journey. For home and library, a vital guide for respectful Jewish/Christian study and spiritual reflection of these shared, transformational sacred narratives."

—RABBI GOLDIE MILGRAM, author of *Reclaiming Bar/Bat Mitzvah
as a Spiritual Rite of Passage*

"In an age where politics and ideologies work to divide us, Rabbi David is a voice in the wilderness calling people of faith to come together by honoring each other and exploring our common roots, stories, and connections. This book offers excellent scholarship and personal insights that will inspire us to dig deeper into the richness of the Exodus event by applying its historical, cultural, personal and religious significance to ourselves. Thank you for this invitation to share in your journey of faith."

—FR. MIKE WALKER, Pastor, St. James Catholic
Church, McMinnville, OR

A Story of Freedom

REIMAGINING
Exodus

Rabbi David Zaslow

PARACLETE PRESS
BREWSTER, MASSACHUSETTS

2017 First Printing

Reimagining Exodus: A Story of Freedom

Copyright © 2017 by David Zaslow

ISBN 978-1-61261-780-0

The Paraclete Press name and logo (dove on cross) are trademarks of Paraclete Press, Inc.

Library of Congress Cataloging-in-Publication Data

Names: Zaslow, David, author.
Title: Reimagining Exodus : a story of freedom / by Rabbi David Zaslow.
Description: Brewster, Massachusetts : Paraclete Press, [2017] | Includes
    bibliographical references.
Identifiers: LCCN 2016056883 | ISBN 9781612617800 (trade paper)
Subjects: LCSH: Bible. Exodus--Criticism, interpretation, etc.
Classification: LCC BS1245.52 .Z37 2017 | DDC 222/.106--dc23
LC record available at https://lccn.loc.gov/2016056883

10 9 8 7 6 5 4 3 2 1

Published by Paraclete Press
Brewster, Massachusetts
www.paracletepress.com

Printed in the United States of America

In memory of my mentor and friend Rabbi Aryeh Hirschfield
and Sister Virginia Shipman of the Sisters of the Holy Names

נחית בחסדך עם זו גאלת נהלת בעזך אל נוה קדשך

In your steadfast love you led the people whom you redeemed;
you guided them by your strength to your holy abode.

EXODUS 15:13

CONTENTS

PART ONE
Exodus—A Way Out

PART TWO
Reimagining Exodus

PART FIVE
Personal Stories

APPENDICES

ACKNOWLEDGMENTS

To my teachers: Rabbi Aryeh Hirschfield, Rabbi Shlomo Carlebach, Rabbi David Wolfe-Blank, and Rabbi Zalman Schachter-Shalomi—may they all be resting in peace beneath the wings of *Shekhinah*. To my interfaith colleagues for their vision: Rev. Anne Bartlett, Rev. Barbara Campbell, and Fr. Mike Walker. To my Havurah Synagogue community in Ashland, Oregon. To my editorial squad: Shoshana Alexander and Dr. Marcia Chaikin for their insightful critiques and suggestions, and especially to Debra Zaslow for her insightful literary editing and excellent sense of order. To Howard Milgram for designing the map of the Exodus journeys. For scholarly feedback from Dr. Rachel Zaslow and Dr. Chioke Ianson. To Jon Sweeney for support for this book. To my editor at Paraclete Press: Phil Fox Rose.

Today, a growing number of us, thank God, do not perceive a competition between Jesus and Torah, between Passover and Easter, between Christianity and Judaism. We no longer accept the false distinction that an angry and judgmental God of the Old Testament was then revealed to be the loving God of the New Testament. Many of us are even beginning to celebrate our differences. I pray that this book is part of that celebration, and I want to acknowledge all the courageous priests, pastors, rabbis, teachers, and scholars who are dedicated to constructing bridges, gates, doors, and windows where once there were only walls.

INTRODUCTION

The Exodus from Egypt, occurring over 3,300 years ago during the reign of Pharaoh Rameses II, is the master story of Judaism. It is an episodic saga made up of dozens of interlocking stories about the return of the Jews to the Promised Land, the land of Canaan, where the children of Jacob had lived, hundreds of years before their enslavement in Egypt. Over the millennia these stories have been interpreted historically, allegorically, and spiritually, and used as archetypal models for dealing with human struggle.

More than a quarter of the world's population holds the story of the Exodus as sacred. Most of the Five Books of Moses (also known as the Pentateuch and Torah) directly relate to the liberation of the children of Israel from slavery. Many of the specific stories are well known: the ten plagues, the burning bush, the crossing of the Red Sea, the revelation at Mount Sinai, the forty years in the wilderness, and so on. The Exodus is, of course, prominent during Passover when Jews relive the journey of their ancestors at seders all over the world and allegorically liberate themselves from personal difficulties. Generation after generation, Jews have reclaimed the Exodus theme in their quests to return from various exiles, including when the nation of Israel was reborn in 1948.

This master story has been appropriated as a template for liberation movements throughout the ages, and, unfortunately, has also been misappropriated by colonial and imperial regimes seeking the conquest of indigenous peoples. The secular world has used the saga to inspire freedom movements around the world, and Christians have used the story to explain Jesus as the Paschal Lamb of a new Passover. The Puritans saw themselves on an exodus from the Egypt of England in their quest for religious freedom. The American revolutionaries used the story in their quest for independence, as did the Mormons in the search for their own promised land in Utah.

The Exodus story served as an inspirational road map for African slaves struggling for freedom from the "pharaohs" of the "American Egypt." Decades later, the Exodus saga was used by the civil rights movement of the 1950s and 1960s. One does not need much imagination to identify the Reverend Martin Luther King Jr. as the Moses of his generation. He too had a vision of justice, freedom, and equal rights as he told the world, "I've been to the mountaintop. . . . And I've looked over. And I've seen the promised land." Like Moses, after powerfully leading his people, he could not enter the land with them.

In order to delve more deeply into the lessons of the Exodus story, we have to define terms that were understood by the children of Israel but may get lost in translation because of the multilayered meanings of biblical Hebrew. For example, the Hebrew word for "bush" in the burning bush encounter, *sneh*, comes from the same root as the word for "Sinai" where the Ten Commandments were given. Does Moses's personal encounter with God in the bush foreshadow his encounter at Sinai on behalf of all the people? Can we see the revelations at the burning bush and at Mount Sinai as reflections of revelatory moments we experience in our own lives?

Exploring the Exodus story more deeply illuminates aspects that are both relevant today and personally inspiring. The Jewish sages and rabbis don't think of Egypt just as the name of a nation where the Hebrews lived at a particular time in history. In Hebrew, Egypt is *Mitzrayim*, meaning "restrictions" or "narrow places." It is often interpreted as an internal, psychological state of confinement. In that same interpretation, the saga of the Hebrews is the set of developmental stages we go through in struggling against our "personal pharaohs." If we imagine the redemption of the Hebrews as a template for our lives, we can use the Exodus as a road map for emerging from the restrictions of our personal "Egypts."

There are a few other Hebrew terms used regularly in this book that need to be defined. For the Five Books of Moses, also called the Pentateuch, I generally use the Hebrew term *Torah*. Because the Bible reads so differently in Hebrew than it does in English, when I use the Hebrew term for the Bible, *Tanakh*, such as, "In the Tanakh it says," I am referring to some subtlety that is only evident in the original. I use the term *Midrash*[1] (plural, *Midrashim*) frequently. It refers to stories, anecdotes, and homiletical commentaries that help us understand the context of a word, verse, commandment, or scene in the Bible. Midrashim are derived from reading between the lines of the text— an interpretative anecdote or story based on what is implied in the Tanakh rather than what is explicitly stated. For instance, in Exodus 10:1 almost all English translations say, "Then the LORD said to Moses, 'Go to Pharaoh'," but the Hebrew does not say "go." It says, "Come to Pharaoh." Why? The Midrash teaches this indicated God would be *there* too.

Common Roots

A primary goal of this book is to bring Jews and Christians closer together to celebrate what we have in common. Judaism and Christianity share the same moral imperative to make our world a better place. The biblical term *yakhdav* describes two people when they are one in purpose, not one in form. The Abrahamic faiths are *yakhdav*, one in purpose with each other—equally vibrant covenantal paths in service to one God. As a religious Jew, I've witnessed the devastation brought about by trium- phalism, when missionaries see themselves as spokespeople for the "one true" religion to which all others must convert. No religion should yield its unique, God-given covenant to the beliefs of a more dominant religion. Whether the theologians of the three Abrahamic faiths acknowledge it or not, our faith traditions provide a harmonious balance to each other— when they are shared in a spirit of mutual respect.

Both Judaism and Christianity are built on the foundation of the exact same stories from the Torah: the Passover and the Exodus. Christians call Jesus the Paschal—or Passover—Lamb, taking the major details of the Exodus saga and allegorically extending them to apply to sin, atonement, forgiveness, salvation, eternal life of the soul, and resurrection of the dead. In the Orthodox Christian Church, Easter is actually called Pascha (Passover, from the Hebrew *Pesach*). When John said of Jesus, "Here is the Lamb of God who takes away the sin of the world" (John 1:29), he was establishing what would become the core of Christian theology. While Judaism does not see Jesus as the Lamb of God, a belief firmly rooted in the ancient pre-rabbinic Judaism of the Tanakh is that the suffering of any innocent soul, including Jesus, has redemptive power.

When my previous book, *Jesus: First-Century Rabbi*, was published by Paraclete Press in 2013, I had used the metaphor from Paul referring to Judaism as the root and the followers of Jesus as the branches. In Romans 11:18, Paul declares, "Do not boast over the branches. If you do boast, remember that it is not you that support the root, but the root that supports you." In an otherwise very positive review, though, Rabbi Brad Hirschfield made an excellent point concerning the root and branch image that I had to seriously consider. He wrote:

> While most Jews, and many Christians, appreciate the apparent advantage of treating Judaism as the elder tradition, as the author does, it is not exactly true. In fact, rabbinic Judaism and Christianity co-arise at roughly the same time, i.e., the first century. . . . Perhaps more productive would be thinking of both Rabbinic Judaism and Christianity as twin children of a common mother—the Hebrew Bible. While that metaphor may offer some unique challenges to both communities, it better represents the actual history of each tradition, and may also help explain some of the enormous pain that has arisen between the two over the centuries.[2]

Rabbi Hirschfield is correct in his critique. After the destruction of the temple in 70 CE, Judaism was completely transformed from an offering-based religion centered around the temple in Jerusalem into the prayer-based faith of rabbinic Judaism. As Christianity was born, so Judaism was reborn. What we now call "rabbinic Judaism" grew up as a sibling to the new monotheistic kid on the block—Christianity. Rather than saying that Judaism and Christianity were "twin children of a common mother—the Hebrew Bible," it might be more accurate to call them twin children of pre-rabbinic Judaism, the Judaism of the Israelites, the Judges, Kings, and Prophets. While Paul's root and branch metaphor was appropriate for his age, it may not be the most accurate metaphor for our era.

In this book, to the dismay of some and the delight of others, Jewish and Christianity theology are afforded mutual respect. The two religions do not espouse the same theology, but neither are their theologies in competition with each other. Are the twin children rivaling, antagonistic, and competitive with each other at times? Yes. Did anti-Semitic slanders come from most of the early church fathers? Yes. Is there a sense within Judaism that its theology is superior? Yes. Do many religious Jews have terrible notions about Jesus and Christianity? Yes. Yet both religions continue to borrow and appropriate best practices and theological ideas from each other, generally without attribution of the source. One goal of this book is to demonstrate how both religions continue to be mutually nourished and sustained by resting on the theological foundation of the Exodus stories.

Throughout the book I refer to replacement theology (also called Supersessionism), which states that the Mosaic covenant of Judaism has been replaced by the new covenant of Christianity. It also holds that Christians have replaced the Jews in their relationship to God. Finally, and most disturbing, it insists that outside of Christianity, no Jew or other non-Christian has a viable means for the remission of sin, atonement with God, and obtaining a place in the world to come. Fortunately, more and more denominations are repudiating this age-old heresy. After almost two thousand years of replacement theology, it is most urgent that we recognize that neither Jesus nor the great evangelist Paul ever taught such exclusivity. In Romans, Paul affirms the theology of Judaism that sustained and gave rise to Christianity.

Protestant scholar Dr. Donald Arthur Carson popularized the saying, "A text without context is a pretext for a proof text."[3] This offers a good warning for people of all faiths not to cite a scriptural text unless we are fully aware of the historical and cultural context in which it was said. The Exodus story began as a uniquely Jewish story, and yet throughout history it has been creatively interpreted and applied to so many different liberation movements. Studying the original story from a Jewish perspective can only enhance the faith of all people who have been inspired by this great episodic saga.

In nature, the Creator has a strict commitment to biodiversity. My teacher Rabbi Zalman Schachter-Shalomi (affectionately known as Reb Zalman—may his memory be a blessing) taught that the principle of biodiversity holds true for religions as well. This is a challenge to the fundamentalists of all faiths, since it means acknowledging truths contained in other belief systems. Consciously or unconsciously, religions see themselves in a doctrinal turf war with each other, and all religions are rightfully afraid of moral relativism where "anything goes." But moral relativism is not the same as theological diversity.

In memory of Reb Zalman, I call the Old Testament and New Testament the Elder Testament and Younger Testament. These titles transform the replacement theology implied by a "new" testament (covenant) replacing the "old." To the Jewish people, the "Old" Testament is still a new and living testament. Using the terms *Elder* and *Younger* is not only mutually respectful but also brings a bit of a smile to our faces. God only knows, Christians and Jews need to smile more when we speak of each other's sacred writings.

In a classic Indian tale, three blindfolded men who have never seen an elephant are put in a room with one and asked to describe the creature. Each man, touching a different part of the elephant, thinks he is describing the whole. Similarly, each religion is perhaps deployed by God to reveal one part of truth, but we're each focusing on describing only the part we're touching. It is my hope that this exploration of the Exodus saga will help us look up from our singular perspectives to gain awareness of the unique but interwoven stories with which our theologies create a unified sense of the divine.

There are many different ways to read the Bible: as literal history or as an outline of history; figuratively, as a collection of archetypes, myths, fables, or metaphors; or as cultural memory. Some read Scripture for its spiritual and moral value regardless of how historically true the stories may be. My goal is not to challenge any particular way of reading sacred texts. I treat the events in the Exodus as true, regardless of their historical veracity. I work with and interpret the Hebrew text of the forty-year Exodus saga without regard as to whether or not it was possible for three million emancipated slaves to have survived together in a semi-arid geographic region like the Sinai Peninsula. Cultural memory, rather than rational analysis, gives me my sense of its truth. I am comfortable living in the mystery—with modern historical inquiry and faith representing different facets of a single truth.

Do we believe the Creation story is true? That God created the world in six twenty-four-hour days and rested on the seventh? Can this be a fact? In the realm of faith and cultural memory, it is true. To account for what modern cosmology proposes—that the cosmos is fifteen-plus billion years old—we'd have to define each day of creation as approximately 2.5 billion years, which could align with the multiple meanings of the word *day* in Hebrew.* There does not need to be an either/or between evolutionism and creationism. I accept the Genesis Creation story and the Big Bang story. It is not one versus the other. Yes and yes. We don't need to let our love of science diminish faith or vice versa.

---

*   The Hebrew word *yom* generally refers to a twenty-four-hour day, but just as in English, it also means the period of daylight hours, as when we say "during the day." In biblical Hebrew, however, the same word is also used to refer to an age, an era, or an ambiguous period of time—perhaps even 2.5 billion years for each *yom*.

Metaphor

The word *metaphor*, derived from ancient Greek roots, means "to carry across." An image from one experience of reality carries us into another. But a metaphor does not operate in physical space with a here and a there, or in time with a now and then. There is nothing to carry. And there is nothing "over there." Yet when I listen to Dylan Thomas invoke the words, "and the Sabbath rang slowly in the pebbles of the holy streams," a part of me understands. I am carried across to a different way of perceiving reality. Literally, the Sabbath does not ring. It is not a bell. And even if it could ring, why should it ring slowly? Why are streams holy, and what are the pebbles? A great metaphor like that carries us over into a different realm, one where it does not have to be factual to be true.

In Psalm 148:3 King David chants, "Praise him, sun and moon; praise him, all you shining stars!" When we read this kind of personification in the Bible, our modern minds tend to reduce David's communication to "just a figure of speech," to being *just* a metaphor. But the metaphor in David's chant is a portal to a level of reality where everything in creation actually does speak to each other in the language God has embedded in every subatomic particle that makes up every galaxy. It's the language of antagonism and reconciliation that we can see in physics and playing out in the natural world.

Poetry—the language of metaphor—transmutes words into pictures and music. In every metaphor an impossible correspondence is made: anything can be described as anything else, and things are said to do what they cannot "really" do. In the hands of the master poets, there is no attempt at trick or illusion in using metaphor—the figure of speech reveals a truth. In our favorite poems, including in the Bible, the lines between the literal and figurative, imaginary and real, rational and spiritual, are blurred. In ancient Hebrew culture, the distinctions between song, metaphor, dance, storytelling, history, prayer, and healing were also blurred.

In biblical Hebrew, there were not clear distinctions between the animate and inanimate world, between the ancestors and us, between nature and our souls. We're all too smart for our own good now— poetry is dead within many of us because we do not live the experience of metaphors. We analyze what they mean instead of seeing them as images or hearing them as music, carrying us over into understanding. We diminish the truth within them when we say, "Oh, that's just a metaphor." The nineteenth-century Christian scholar E. W. Bullinger compiled an authoritative work on the use of metaphor and figurative language in the Bible. He understood the connection between metaphor and truth, between the image and its reflection. In 1899, declaring that biblical figures of speech are one of the most important areas of Bible study, he wrote:

> A passage of God's Word is quoted; and is met with the cry, "Oh, that is figurative"—implying that its meaning is weakened, or that it has quite a different meaning, or that it has no meaning at all. But the very opposite is the case. . . . In fact, it is not too much to say that in the use of these figures, we have, as it were, the Holy Spirit's own markings in our Bible. . . . It is clear, therefore, that no branch of Bible-study can be more important: and yet we may truly say that there is no branch of it which has been so utterly neglected.[4]

To the Hebrews—and to many indigenous people today—metaphor and reality go hand in hand; the imaginal realm and the observable realm are partners; physicality and spirituality are two sides of a single coin; history and theology are intimately linked. Interpretation of a sacred text can be enriched when we understand that an embedded truth is revealed when we let a metaphor take us. It may not be "true" on one level of reality but it is profoundly true on a deeper level. God uses a metaphor when declaring, "The mountains and the hills before you shall burst into song, and all the trees of the field shall clap their hands" (Isa. 55:12). Asking whether mountains can sing or trees can clap misses the point. Taking in the metaphor brings us closer to God and to the created world.

An authentic metaphor is not a clever, fanciful, but essentially unreal figure of speech. Rather, it is a description arising from the deepest depths—not unreality but the very essence of reality. Great poets, biblical and contemporary, do not use a metaphor to express their imaginations; they use it as the only way they can approximate the truth—a snapshot of the miraculous. May we all be blessed to return to seeing and hearing the world and the cosmos with fewer boundaries and fewer lines of distinction!

Etymology

Etymology, the study of word origins, is a window into history. In the ancient origin of a word, we may discover an analogy that people used hundreds or thousands of years ago to express themselves or understand the world around them. Etymology is really the archeology of language. It reveals the past with a fascinating form of historical evidence—the metaphor.

It reveals the root metaphors the word's coiner would have imagined. For example, the word *window* comes from Old Norse for "eye of the wind." The animate "wind" was given an "eye" when someone in the twelfth century built a house. The word *intellect* comes from the Latin *inter* + *legere*, meaning "to choose between." Using the "intellect" was seen as an act of "choosing" to the Romans. When we apply the study of word origins of proper names in the Bible, an entirely new layer of metaphorical interpretation becomes possible, giving the biblical stories a new dimension.

In Hebrew, words have multiple meanings, which allows for a beautiful array of "literal" translations to arise from a single biblical word or passage. For example, the journey from Egypt to Canaan becomes one from a place of "restrictions" to a place of "being in humility."

The Hebrew word for Egypt is *Mitzrayim*, from a root word meaning "restrictions." This referred to the fertile double-delta region in northern Egypt created by the branching of the Nile River as it comes close to the Mediterranean Sea. The geological plains of the delta are restricted by this branching. Later, in Jewish theology the word *mitzrayim* was applied metaphorically to a state of psychological enslavement. The name *Canaan* comes from a root meaning "lowland"—named for the low elevation of the land on the Mediterranean side of the Jordan River. The same root gives rise to the sense of "to be humbled" or "to fall on one's knees."

At the etymological level there is no such thing as an abstract word. All words were originally concrete and visual, and this is especially true of biblical Hebrew and of the ancient Hebrew people themselves. The mid-twentieth-century Bible scholar Dr. Mary Ellen Chase put it this way:

> The associative powers of [the Hebrew] mind and its intensely emotional character were perpetually endowing the simple and the obvious with their inner and spiritual significance, forever transcending the familiar and the ordinary. Thus the literal becomes the figurative as well; the concrete loses its sharp outlines in the abstract. Nothing is seen alone, but is forever attended by its meaning, like a surrounding light or a reflected shadow.[5]

There are different types of etymological studies that are useful for examining the origins of biblical words. Lexicons and biblical commentaries yield both scholarly word studies and imaginative speculations. Etymological assertions are in an ongoing state of correction and modification as archeology and historical research reveal new evidence about the origins of particular words. For linguists, the goal is simply to uncover the historical past, but for theologians, it is to make a biblical text more meaningful in the lives of the faithful.

PART ONE

Exodus—A Way Out

The Exodus from Egypt in Hebrew: *Yetziat Mitzrayim*

*E*xodus in English usage means one of two things. First, as a proper noun it describes the Exodus of the Hebrews who were redeemed from hundreds of years of enslavement in Egypt. The word is also used when any large population is on the move, due to either liberation or exile—as we've seen with African Americans leaving the South in the early part of the twentieth century, and Syrian refugees fleeing their embattled homeland in the early part of the twenty-first century. For the former, it was a search for opportunity and justice; for the latter, an escape in desperation.

Yetziah — Exodus

The English word *exodus* is derived from the Greek *ex*, meaning "out," and *hodos*, meaning "way"—the "way out." For the children of Israel, the Exodus was a way out of enslavement. The phrase *yetziat Mitzrayim* as used in Jewish liturgy refers to "the exodus from Egypt," but *y'tziah* is a common word akin to "departure" or "exit." It appears in hundreds of ways in the Hebrew Bible, often figuratively. In Genesis 1:12, *y'tziah* is used to describe the earth as having "brought forth" vegetation—poetically speaking, vegetation is making an "exodus" from its primal earth-bound seed state. In Genesis 1:24, the earth "brings forth living creatures" using the same verb. Whether it's the rivers *coming out* of Eden (Gen. 2:10); the raven *going forth* from Noah's ark (Gen. 8:7); the sun *rising* (Gen. 19:23); or bread being *brought forth* from the earth, the same word in Hebrew is used to describe the action. Each is an *exodus* from a kind of restriction.

Mitzrayim — Egypt

In the imagination of the Talmudic sages, *Mitzrayim* was not just the nation from which the Jews were set free at a particular time in history; it also was the act of being set free from psychological enslavement. The "pharaoh" of this internal *Mitzrayim* may be a real person causing restriction, or it may be a limiting component of an individual's personality. For example, we are in *Mitzrayim* when we are in a harmful relationship, or if self-doubt is unduly limiting us. A personal state of *Mitzrayim* can be described as having restricted access to both God and self. *Mitzrayim* is discussed in these psychological terms by many rabbis each year before Passover. One of the great twentieth-century teachers, Rabbi Menachem Schneerson explains the connection between the historical Exodus and the exoduses we experience many times during our lives:

> The exodus from Egypt was not only a physical liberation from outside forces of enslavement, imprisonment and "limitation," but also . . . from their own "straits"—their bad habits and inclinations. This inner liberation took many progressive stages, many "journeys," and each journey was an exodus from the "Egypt"—the limitation—of the previous stage. For today's accomplishments in self-liberation from evil are tomorrow's "Egypt." Yesterday the person freed himself, to a certain degree, from his former unwholesome traits, he left Egypt. But today he cannot be satisfied with yesterday's standards of accomplishment. Not only is yesterday's liberation from evil insufficient, imperfect—it is, for today, a strait, a limitation, an Egypt from which an exodus must be experienced.[6]

The Jewish experience in Egypt can be studied and interpreted on historic, symbolic, allegorical, and psychological levels. Examining the

Exodus story as a prototype for all our personal journeys is one primary way that such an ancient liberation saga continues to have profound meaning in our lives today for Jews and non-Jews alike.

Correcting Our Image of the Exodus

In popular culture we often imagine the Exodus as the children of Israel walking in circles and wandering a barren desert for forty years. Many of the images we have about the "wanderings" of the newly freed Hebrew slaves are inaccurate.

First, they weren't in the kind of desert we might imagine, with sand dunes and an almost empty landscape. If we examine the map of the forty-two campsites (see *The Map of the Exodus & 42 Wilderness Journeys* on page 37) along the Exodus route (enumerated in Numbers 33:1–49), we see that at almost all times the Hebrews were within a few miles of fresh water for bathing, refreshment, and certainly for fish. The Sinai Peninsula is a section of what geologists call the Great Rift Valley that sits between the Gulf of Suez to the west, and the Gulf of Aqaba to the east—both tributaries of the Red Sea. What we call the "desert" is, in both Hebrew and Arabic, the *Arabah* (the root of the words *Arab* and *Arabia*), meaning a plain or steppe. Although hot and dry, the *Arabah* is known for its beautiful, colored cliffs, ancient rock paintings, and some of the oldest copper mines in the world. Rather than *desert*, a better translation of *arabah* is "wilderness."

Families in the Sinai region earn their livelihood from sheep herding, light agriculture, and fishing, much as they might have done at the time of the Exodus. It is not unlike some areas in New Mexico where Native American tribes have thrived for centuries. The *Arabah* is a unique, delicate ecosystem made up of plants and animals living in a sparse, hot environment. It has abundant resources, including fresh water springs and the saltwater gulfs they feed that surround the land on three sides.

Second, the children of Israel were not lost or moving about randomly for forty years—meandering nomads following an erratic path on their way to the Promised Land. Most of the time the Hebrews lived in highly organized family or clan campsites, aligned according to tribes around a portable tabernacle they built during the Exodus. Except for the first and last years of the Exodus, on average they stayed in each location for more than a year. Some sages have suggested they lived in one of the locations for as many as nineteen of the forty years. Rather than wandering aimlessly, it seems likely that, under the leadership of Moses, Aaron, and Miriam, the nation was waiting for its younger generation to gain the skills and courage they would need to defend it against hostile tribes when they returned to settle Canaan.

It is important also to grasp how relatively small the distances are. From the Egyptian city of Rameses, where the newly freed slaves assembled to leave Egypt, to Mount Sinai is approximately 250 miles. From Sinai to the border of Canaan at the Jordan River is around 250 miles. In forty years, they traveled about 500 miles, stopping at forty-two campsites along the way, each about ten to twenty miles apart from each other. With the slow movement of a large population with children and livestock, the Hebrews had more than a generation to psychologically prepare for life as free men and women.

A third incorrect impression we have of the Exodus is that up to three million men, women, and children left Egypt at once and followed Moses all at the same time. Ecologically, the *Arabah* would not have been able to withstand so many people all crowded together in campsites. Also, from what we now know, large emigration is usually spread out over a number of years.[7] Some historians suggest that the forty years of the Exodus may instead actually mark the four decades it took the Hebrews to *leave* Egypt—wave after wave, year after year, following several different routes depending on when they left. This makes more sense.

In the story of the twelve spies (Numbers 12) the Torah indicates that the people were too afraid to enter the land of Canaan when they arrived at the end of the first year, and that the forty years in the wilderness was a punishment from God for their self-doubt, lack of faith, and timidity. As a result, the liberated Hebrew slaves, except for Caleb and Joshua and the younger generation, would all die in the wilderness.

It's important to know also that the route Moses took was intentional and intelligently planned. First, it avoided hostile tribes that would have confronted them had Moses led them by the short route along the Mediterranean Sea. Second, following what today we call the Gulf of Suez and the Gulf of Aqaba, the route was near water and would give them time to develop a strategy for returning to Canaan, where the tribes of Jacob originated hundreds of years earlier.

The Centrality of the Exodus

Most Jewish rituals are intended to be a reminder of the Exodus. Why do Jews keep the festivals? As a reminder of the Exodus from Egypt. Why do Jews wear head coverings? Prayer shawls? As a reminder of the Exodus from Egypt. All three pilgrimage festivals—Passover (*Pesakh* in Hebrew), Pentecost (*Shavuot* in Hebrew), and Tabernacles (*Succoth* in Hebrew)—have been interpreted to relate to the Exodus. Rabbi Irving Greenberg says that:

> Passover, marking the liberation, and *Sukkot* (Tabernacles) commemorating the journey, are the alpine events in the Hebrew calendar. *Shavuot* (Pentecost) is the link between the two major Exodus commemorations, marking the transformation of Exodus from a one-time event into an ongoing commitment.[8]

When Jews welcome the Sabbath on Friday evening with the kiddush (sanctification of wine), the prayer asks the participants to remember two things: (1) the work of creation and (2) the Exodus from Egypt. The Exodus is such a central theme and trope in Judaism that it is actually paired and intertwined with the creation of the universe. Here is an excerpt from the traditional kiddush recited every Friday:

> Blessed are You Holy One, our God, Sovereign of the Universe . . .
> In Your love and favor You have made the holy Sabbath
> our heritage, as a reminder of the work of creation.
> It is first among our sacred days,
> and a remembrance of the Exodus from Egypt . . .
> Blessed are You, Holy One, who sanctifies the Sabbath.

On a mystical level, the redemption of the Hebrews was a reiteration of the Creation story but with human characters and plots. As the cosmos is created from what Genesis 1:2 describes as a state of *tohu* and *bohu*—formlessness and emptiness—so slavery was a kind of formless and empty existence for the Hebrews. Yet out of the constriction of enslavement came the awareness that it was a sole deity who brought about the liberation. Out of the liberation came the creation and birth of a new nation, a new understanding of divinity, and ultimately a new religion.

The forty-year Exodus experience in the wilderness was the laboratory out of which emerged the Judaism we know today—a Judaism based on a few core principles: love your neighbor as yourself (Lev. 19:18); love God with all your heart (Deut. 6:5); and live by faith (Hab. 2:4). These principles arose from the foundational belief that we all are created in the divine image (Gen. 1:26) and descended from common ancestors. Both Jews and Christians are assured by God that they can fulfill their covenantal obligations through the practice of sacred remembrance—the Passover seder and Sabbath in Judaism, and the Eucharist in Christianity.

The Exodus is a saga that begins with enslavement and culminates in liberation, followed fifty days later by the revelation of the Ten Commandments at Mount Sinai. The main part of the Exodus culminates in the death of Moses, and Joshua leading the people into the Promised Land. Then, settled in Canaan, the Hebrews became a nation for the first time, and like all nations they struggled against internal corruption, religious disputes, and invasions from outside empires. This part can be broadly defined as the age of the judges, kings, and prophets. The final part of the Exodus never ends—it is an ongoing journey as it unfolds in the drama of enslavement and liberation in each person's life. While I call the Exodus an archetype, I appreciate journalist Krista Tippett's redefining the word *myth* to its original meaning. She writes:

> Exodus . . . qualifies lavishly for my favorite definition of "myth"—a word we've diminished, equated with things that

are not "true." Myth, said the Greek statesman Solon, "is not about something that never happened. It is about something that happens over and over again." In a paraphrase I also love, Rabbi Sandy Sasso once said to me about the Exodus story, with its irresistible dramatic potential: "What happened once upon a time happens all the time."[9]

Dr. Abigail E. Gillman uses an elegant metaphor, coined by French historian Pierre Nora, to frame the Exodus. She writes, "The biblical narrator recorded the Exodus story not as myth, nor as chronicle, but as a *lieu de memoire*, a layered, conflicted, constructed site of memory."[10] Rabbi Lawrence Kushner also asks us to see the Exodus in very personal, psychological terms. In his classic guidebook to the Torah, *The River of Light*, he writes, "Reconsider the going out from Egypt. Not as an historical event or even a mythic one. But as the story of the transformation of consciousness."[11]

Each Passover Jewish families recite the story of the Exodus from the liturgical guidebook called the Haggadah. Before the festive meal begins, families gather to recreate a *lieu de memoire*, a sense of living history in response to four questions ceremonially chanted by the youngest child in the family. These begin with the question, "Why is this night different from all other nights?" and an adult in the family answers:

> We were slaves of Pharaoh in Egypt, and the Lord our God brought us out from there with a mighty hand and an outstretched arm. Now, if God had not brought our forebears out of Egypt, then even we, our children, and our children's children might still be enslaved to Pharaoh in Egypt.

It really is an astounding bit of sacred hyperbole to think that "we, our children, and our children's children might still be enslaved to Pharaoh in Egypt." After 3,300 years I'm not sure we'd literally still be slaves, but I am convinced there would be no Judaism, Christianity, or Islam without the hallowed obligation to remember and retell the Passover story year after year. The result of this yearly family remembrance ritual, practiced in evolving forms for three millennia, is that Jews believe the revelation of Torah came out of the anguish of enslavement.

The universal vision of the prophets made it easy to turn the Exodus into a template for liberation and justice for people throughout world. This template is clearly at the foundation of Christianity as well. Historian Dr. David Brion Davis reminds us of how central the model of the Exodus continues to be in Western civilization:

> The story has been recapitulated and transmogrified not only in the Old and New Testaments but also through much of Western history. It has conveyed the astounding message that in the past God actually heard the cries of the *oppressed* and was willing to free slaves from their masters. Indeed, God passed over the brilliant and powerful peoples of the ancient Near East and chose a group of degraded slaves to bear the awesome responsibility of receiving and transmitting his law. Exodus has therefore furnished a model for every kind of deliverance, whether by escape, revolution, or spiritual rebirth.[12]

Interpretative Differences: Exodus and Law

Christian scholar Dr. Scott M. Langston in his important book *Exodus Through the Centuries* reminds us: "Christians have used Exodus from a dramatically different vantage point, understanding Israel's biblical exodus in light of Jesus' life, death, and resurrection. Jesus, who through his death and resurrection made possible the exodus from slavery to sin, is consistently understood as the Passover Lamb of God."[13] This difference, I believe, is divinely sanctioned. As the French say, "vive la différence!" God loves diversity. After 2,000 years, Jews and Christians are increasingly coming to the realization that these two stories, of Judaism and Christianity, are not at odds with each other; nor is one a prefiguration or completion of the other. Rather, they are complementary stories recorded in two different historic periods and made sacred within two different religions.

However, Dr. Langston cautions us to remember, "…despite their general acceptance of the historicity of the Exodus, most Christians throughout history have been interested less in the Exodus as a historical event as how the Exodus can elevate the distinctive features of their own faith."[14] Drawing distinctions is a good thing, of course, but all too often the story of Jesus as the Paschal Lamb has been used to promote replacement theology in declaring that the purpose of the Exodus had been "fulfilled," meaning further that the commandment to observe the Passover is no longer in effect. The church fathers are particularly clear that the Passover story is important but only as a prefiguration of the Christ story. Dr. John Coffey, professor of history at the University of Leicester, summarizes the teachings of the church fathers:

For [Origen] and other early Church Fathers, the Exodus foreshadowed the redemption from spiritual bondage wrought by the Messiah. Christ was the Passover Lamb whose blood protected believers as the angel of death passed over Egypt. He was the new Moses who led his people out of the Egypt of demonic slavery and through the wilderness of this life. He was the Joshua who brought them across the Jordan of death and into the Promised Land of Heaven.[15]

Paul's discourse in Galatians has been used by those espousing replacement theology to prove that the law (the 613 commandments of the Torah that are observed in Judaism) is no longer necessary. Whether Paul's statement has been interpreted correctly or not, it certainly has been used as a foundational text to justify the argument for the replacement of the Mosaic covenant with a new and "better covenant" (Heb. 8:6). Paul says in Galatians 3:23–26:

> We were imprisoned and guarded under the law until faith would be revealed. Therefore the law was our disciplinarian until Christ came, so that we might be justified by faith. But now that faith has come, we are no longer subject to a disciplinarian, for in Christ Jesus you are all children of God through faith.

Throughout history, loyalty to the Torah and God's commandments has comforted and inspired the Jewish people; it is the primary reason Judaism has survived in a hostile world. Paul refers to the law as a disciplinarian, but in Judaism the Torah is our beloved friend, our partner in defining the covenantal obligations prescribed by the Holy One of Israel. In the late 1970s, Rabbi Abraham Joshua Heschel summed up the Jewish loyalty to the Torah this way:

How grateful I am to God that there is a duty to worship, a law to remind my distraught mind that it is time to think of God, time to disregard my ego for at least a moment! It is such happiness to belong to an order of the divine will. I am not always in a mood to pray. I do not always have the vision and the strength to say a word in the presence of God. But when I am weak, it is the law that gives me strength; when my vision is dim, it is duty that gives me insight.[16]

Where Does the Exodus Begin?

At what point in time does the Exodus saga begin? If by *exodus* we mean "departure," then on the simplest level we'd all agree that the Exodus began the morning after the first Passover. That's when the Hebrews began their journey into the wilderness on the way back to Canaan. But the actual Exodus story began long before the emancipation of the slaves. Maybe we'd be wiser to mark the beginning of the Exodus story with the return of Moses to Egypt after living in Midian for forty years. The Torah and tradition tell us that at eighty years of age he returns to the land of his birth and confronts Pharaoh, the stepbrother he grew up with, uttering the famous words, "Let my people go!"

However, the story begins even before that. The start of Moses's return to Egypt can be pinpointed to the moment when he encounters God at the burning bush. It is there, at that miraculous site in the wilderness, where Moses receives the order from God to return to Egypt and to become the liberator of his people. Yet somehow even that beginning does not satisfy the curious mind, which asks, "But how did the Hebrews who came from Canaan hundreds of years earlier get enslaved in the first place?" To answer that we have to go back to the story of Joseph, the Hebrew son of Jacob, who miraculously became the viceroy of Egypt under an earlier Pharaoh.

You see the dilemma? We keep going back in the Bible looking for the beginning, and each time we've found one, we are confronted with the fact that for every beginning there seems to be an earlier beginning. Maybe the start of the Exodus saga begins with Abraham and Sarah when God commands them, hundreds of years before the actual Exodus, to leave the city of Ur in Mesopotamia and journey to a land that the Almighty would show them—the land of Canaan. Or maybe it begins with Adam and Eve when they are commanded to leave the Garden of Eden to begin life with all the challenges and struggles that being human brings. In a profound way the Creation story itself is a kind of exodus, an exodus *ex nihilo*, a departure from nothingness to somethingness. Can we say that the creation of the material world is a kind of liberation, God's own self-liberation from the empty void of the pre-Creation? Is that possible?

For a moment let's ask the question in the other direction. Where does the Exodus end? Does it come to an end when the new generation crosses the Jordan River and enters the Promised Land? Does the Exodus end when we finish reading the book of Deuteronomy? Or does a new journey, a different kind of exodus begin? Not an exodus out of slavery, but an exodus out of the fear and self-doubt displayed by the spies when they returned to Moses with an "evil report." Does the Exodus end when each of the twelve tribes settles in their apportioned sections of land? Or hundreds of years later when King Solomon builds the temple in Jerusalem, creating a physical place in which the Jewish people can celebrate the three harvest pilgrimage festivals—Passover, Pentecost, and Tabernacles?

Once the Israelites settled in Canaan they began a new stage in the Exodus saga living on the land of their ancestors as farmers, ranchers, merchants, craftspeople, teachers, religious leaders, healers, and judges. They were about to become adults, fully responsible for caring for the land and each other, and fully able to follow the commandments God gave them at Sinai. Is that where the Exodus ends? Maybe it ends when the Jewish people return to the Holy Land after the Persian king Cyrus underwrites the rebuilding of the second temple. Maybe the Exodus ends in 1948 with the reestablishment of Israel after the Holocaust.

By asking these questions we find a secret answer to the Exodus riddle. Everything we say about the ancient Jewish people is true for each of us as an individual; the Exodus never really ends but is an ongoing process of God's liberation in every individual, ritually reenacted at every Passover celebration. The final stage of the Exodus, the real battle that Joshua fought at Jericho, is inside of us. The walls that "come tumblin' down" are the walls of ignorance, fear, and prejudice. Each of us has the opportunity to enter our own Promised Land. God wants us to trumpet our way into Jericho and come home. God wants us to reach a higher level of social responsibility as quickly as possible. But first we must take responsibility and move our way through the stages of the Exodus—one journey at a time.

Over the five centuries following the destruction of the temple in Jerusalem, the sages of the Talmud reinvented Judaism from a religion based on bringing offerings of fruit, grain, and animals to the temple to a religion based upon another kind of offering—prayer, the "fruit of our lips" (Hos. 14:2). The rabbis reimagined in increasing detail the connection between the historical Exodus and its personal application to individuals and the nation.

After their liberation from slavery, the entire Exodus story was understood as a lens through which the Jewish people could make sense of their ongoing plight among the nations. Pharaoh was reinterpreted as the internal, reactionary force holding people back from their divinely appointed destiny. At the same time, Pharaoh was not just spiritualized. He was seen symbolically as the embodiment of despotic leaders that the Jewish people would encounter in their various exiles, including the diaspora after the destruction of the Jerusalem temple in 70 CE. Hebrew Bible scholar Dr. Pamela Barmash sums it up beautifully:

> *Exodus!* No other event in Jewish history has so captured the emotions and thoughts of Jews throughout the millennia like the Exodus. . . . The rites of Passover have been shaped and reshaped as Jews have faced the exigencies of exile and the corresponding challenges of intellect and spirit. In so doing, Jews have refashioned the story of the Exodus and the rituals of Passover by means of innovative religious, social and cultural strategies . . . the Exodus has functioned as the primary hermeneutical model from which Jews have created theological meaning and historical self-understanding.[17]

Entry into Canaan was a new beginning for the emancipated slaves, but the Promised Land was not seen as an end point. The moment they arrived, the groundwork for a new beginning, a new kind of journey, began to take shape. Jewish tradition teaches that every morning is a springtime of the day, a liberation from the death of sleep as we awaken to the freedoms and responsibilities of each new day. We should think of the Exodus as a verb and not a noun. We should think of it as both a historical event and an archetypal allegory, as a process not a product, ongoing and never-ending.

Passover: A Leap of Faith

All religions interpret their scriptures on multiple levels. Jews generally interpret stories in the Tanakh using a method called *Pardes*. A verse or story can be interpreted on any of four levels: (1) as an account of the creation of the world and formation of the Jewish people, (2) as a moral guideline for all people, (3) as an allegory that can be applied to other situations throughout history, and (4) as a psychological template for understanding ourselves. Each of these four levels of interpretation is relevant in different situations at different times. When we examine the state of the world today, for example, we might apply the moral or allegorical level of interpretation. When we examine our own lives, we might interpret the stories looking for the "personal message" that God wants each of us to receive. Christianity, of course, also uses a multilevel method for biblical interpretation.

During Passover many Jews look at the Exodus story in relation to their own state of freedom. Although the bondage of the Hebrews ended long ago, on an emotional level the story speaks to each person today. At seder meals around the world, Jews ask questions like: "How am I enslaved now? Who is my inner Moses? Miriam? Elijah? Pharaoh? How can I personally relate to the ten plagues? Where is the path that will lead me out of Egypt? What will happen when I am free?"

The name *Passover* is derived from the story of the evening before the liberation when the Hebrews were told to paint the blood of their lamb offering on their doorposts so the angel of death would "pass over" their dwellings. In Hebrew, Passover is *Pesakh*, and the word is derived from the gamboling, skipping movement of lambs. It is likely that the Passover story of the Hebrews became associated with two much older festivals, celebrations of the barley harvest and lambing season—the angel of death skipping over the Hebrew dwellings being associated with the liberating feelings that springtime elicits, with a carefree attitude, a "skipping over" of obstacles.

When we leap over an obstacle the implication is that the obstacle is still there. On the metaphoric journey we make from slavery to freedom, sometimes we don't eliminate our obstacles, we simply leap over them. Maybe the term "a leap of faith" (*saltus fidei* in Latin) is related to this idea since an act of faith often requires that we leap over some doubt. How do I get out of my chains, habits, and negative attitudes? How do I remove myself from the forces of the pharaoh within me? The spiritual question each Jew asks during the Passover season is "How do I get out of my private *Mitzrayim*, my own Egypt, my own restricted narrow place?" The answer may be in our biology.

We might look at the baby's first major journey—the process of birth—to understand what it means for a baby to pass through a narrow birth canal into a world where gravity is at play. From birth on, movement and change will never be easy and will be affected by the memory of the birth process. Modern psychology holds that our first journey has a powerful effect on our destiny and is a determinant factor in the way we handle problems and challenges throughout our lives. The challenge of the birth journey has been called "birth trauma," but "birth exodus" might be a better term since *trauma* implies something harmful. Birth and death are the two most powerful human experiences; they bookend life. Analogously, the Exodus story begins with the birth of Moses and ends with his death. All experiences during life fit into the template of what our souls "remember" from birth—the struggle to be born. In the same way, the experiences of the Jewish people fit into the template of what its collective soul remembers from the Exodus.

In this same manner, the doorways that God commands the Israelites to smear with blood can be understood to symbolize the birth process. A doorway is, after all, a point of transition from one world to another. Each time a person leaves home, it is a kind of birth into the world. Since the word *Egypt* in Hebrew means "restrictions," most rabbis today teach that the restrictions of Egypt became a kind of birth canal through which the Hebrews were to be born as a new nation. Out of that narrow place of enslavement, Judaism would eventually be born. Historian Dr. David Biale takes this analogy further:

> National birth, much like individual births (and all the more so in ancient times), takes place on a delicate border between life and death. It involves the transformation of blood from a signifier of death to a signifier of life. It also involves the successful opening of the womb, the prevention of the womb's turning into a grave.[18]

In commenting on that night when the angel of death passed over the homes of the Hebrews, Dr. Abigail E. Gillman makes the direct connection between the dwelling places of the slaves to the birth of the nation: "In the course of a single night, the slave dwelling became a Jewish home, the house of bondage turned into a place of collective celebration and ritual observance, and the nation was birthed as God's first offspring."[19] Biblical scholar Dr. Scott Langston offers us the spiritual interpretation of the doorposts from the fourth-century church theologian Gregory of Nyssa who "finds in the application of the blood to the lintel and doorposts a key to understanding the soul and its journey toward virtue. The two doorposts represent the spirit and the appetite, while the lintel reflects the soul's intellect or reason."[20]

The nineteenth-century theologian Rabbi Samson Raphael Hirsch interpreted the two doorposts and the lintel as representing protection by God from the forces of society and nature. He wrote:

> The two door posts represent shutting out the social element; the lintel represents the protection against the physical elements. The slaves when elevated to free human beings with full human rights over their own family life received insurance

by God of their protection against intrusion by the forces of man and nature:[21]

Dr. Abigail Gillman's unpacking of Rabbi Hirsch's teaching deepens this understanding:

> From the vantage point of the Israelites on the ground, the blood ostensibly signaled both the horizontal and vertical dimensions of God's power. Hirsch observes that the blood above, on the lintel, denotes both the natural world—all that which rained down from above in the months prior to this first month—and the supernatural Being who pulls the strings, whereas the blood on the doorposts highlights the revolution taking place in the social domain, in the household, the family, the community, the nation.[22]

The Passover celebration of the Exodus is calibrated to match what people in temperate climates already experience in springtime—they feel the need to get outside, to be free and liberated. Yearning to experience love in the spring, the rabbis instituted the reading of the Song of Songs in the Passover season. Pesach is a marker for what is already happening biologically and in nature. The seder dinner is not just a reenactment of a historical event, but a dress rehearsal for what the participants are each going to do with their newfound freedom in the weeks after the festival.

During Yom Kippur, the Day of Atonement in the autumn, Jews do deep inner work. A litany of sins are confessed and mistakes are acknowledged in what is called an "inventory of the soul." Negative behavioral patterns are assessed in a careful, methodical process. Each internal, psychological item is marked with a label: keep, discard, revise, or change. New vows are made. This is not the case during the Passover season. The work of Pesach is carefree and easy, almost careless. The image of the Lord with a mighty hand and an outstretched arm lifting every generation out of Egypt offers an inspiring template for new possibilities.

After the angel of death passed over the Hebrew dwellings at midnight, they quickly cleaned their houses and prepared to be set free. No hesitation. The dawn came quickly too. They left in haste. There was no time for inventory and careful self-analysis. Dawn was the time to leap, to skip over their uncertainty and take the next step. Today we apply the story like this: Do I have a problem or old habit I want to change? A negative behavioral pattern? Take a chance and jump over it! Make the leap to a new way of being.

Passover is a time for independent action; Jews trust that unseen, godly forces in the universe will be the underlying, driving force that delivers them to freedom. In spring, the people look outward, and seeing the hand of God, they trust that redemption is at hand, everything is possible.

A Christian once asked my teacher Reb Zalman, "Are Jews saved by faith or works?" He answered, "From the Day of Atonement to Passover, from autumn through winter we're saved by works. From Passover to the Jewish New Year, from spring through summer we're saved by faith." The Younger Testament affirms the Jewish view that sees a balance between our works and our faith. James said, "For just as the body without the spirit is dead, so faith without works is also dead" (Jas. 2:26). We need both faith and works. In autumn we make the preparations for a long winter. Food and supplies are prepared and stored. During springtime we have faith that God's grace will once again descend and express itself in the rebirth of nature. Just wait, and the bounty of the land and trees will feed us.

It's not a choice of faith or works. It's both. And each one in its time and proper season—sometimes faith, sometimes works, sometimes both. Doing it yourself—pursuing atonement through repentance—that's the work of autumn. Leaving it to God—that's the faith that comes with spring when rebirth seems to happen by itself. It's in spring that we can leap over the obstacles; liberation, renewal, and birth in nature seem to happen all by themselves. In springtime, God's voice says, "Make the change, take the leap! Skip over fear. Pass over self-doubt."

Developmental Models
Applied to the Exodus

Hebrews, Israelites, and Jews

The terms *Hebrews, Israelites*, and *Jews* are often used synonymously, but historically they represent three distinct time frames in Jewish history. They overlap by as much as several hundred years, so the terms cannot be relied upon for precision. But I have taken the liberty of treating them as three distinct time periods, and as a generalization it works.

Jews were called Hebrews from the time of Abraham through the enslavement in Egypt. They became Israelites as they settled Canaan and the northern Kingdom of Israel. Much later when the southern Kingdom of Judea became dominant, they were called Jews. The etymologies of these three names reveal a poetic and nonhistorical pattern in the evolution of Judaism.

The name *Hebrew* is derived from *Ivrim* (or *Ibrim*), people "from the other side," because Abraham, Sarah, and their descendants had roots on the eastern side of the Jordan River outside of Canaan. The *Ivrim* were metaphorically "boundary crossers," a term coined by Rabbi Gershon Winkler. The *Ivrim* built cultural bridges between the great cultures of Mesopotamia, Canaan, and Egypt.

The word *Israel* means "wrestled with God" and comes from the time when Jacob wrestled with an angel of God and was renamed Israel because he had "striven with God and with humans" and had prevailed (Gen. 32:28). Many rabbis today translate the term *Israel* as "people who wrestle with God," or, as Rabbi Arthur Waskow calls the Jewish people, "Godwrestlers." The term *Israelites* generally designates the people after they settled in Canaan.

The term *Jew* comes from Judah, one of Jacob's older sons for whom one of the twelve tribes was named. The name is derived from the Hebrew word for "gratitude" or "praise." It became a more common designation of the Jewish people starting at the time of the later prophets, or after the end of the Babylonian exile around 536 BCE. The word *Jew* is used regularly in the book of Esther. Metaphorically, a Hebrew is a "boundary crosser," an Israelite is a *"God-wrestler,"* and a Jew is one who gives *"praise."* These three designations form a poetic way to describe the development of the Jewish people before and after the Exodus.

Developmental Design in the Exodus

There was a lot of emotional and cultural development among the children of Israel during the forty-year wilderness period of the Exodus. Part of it had to do with a natural generational change, from the liberated slaves to a younger generation born in freedom. A developmental pattern seems to emerge when we examine the cultural growth of the Hebrews during that time. A larger pattern emerges when we study the entire history of Judaism.

The Exodus we read about in the books of Exodus, Numbers, and Deuteronomy encompasses all the ups and downs of generational transition. The older generation of liberated slaves could not enter the Promised Land because of their "I can't do it" mentality that came from hundreds of years of subjugation. Their incessant grumbling, lack of gratitude, and fantasies about the good life "back in Egypt" were understandable but incompatible with the miracles they were experiencing. We learn in the Torah that on several occasions it took Moses's intercession to convince God not to destroy the complaining, murmuring, and rebelling children of Israel. In the book of Deuteronomy, we see the emotional growth of the population, as Moses recounts the Exodus story to a new generation preparing itself to enter Canaan under Joshua.

The experiences of the Hebrews during the Exodus do not flow in an orderly sequence. Things seem quite random, until viewed from a macro perspective. For every two steps forward they made coming out of slavery, they took one step back. This mixture of orderly, chaotic, and random sequences can be seen as a reflection of all developmental processes, including our personal journeys.

The newly liberated slaves could not have seen the big picture of which they were part. How could they possibly know that they were the stars, co-stars, and the entire cast and crew of this epic Exodus reality series? They just followed the order from dawn to dusk, wrapped within seasons contained within years, for a total of four decades. Each journey and each experience must have been bewildering to them. They had no idea they were part of the greatest collective liberation story ever told.

It's natural for the modern reader to want to find an orderly developmental progression in the forty-two journeys summarized in Numbers 33. We want to discover an embedded "twelve-step program to revelation," or a "forty-two step road map to the Promised Land." But life is not so easy to chart. The Hebrews were just "Hebrew-ing"—they were not trying to create a perfect blueprint that future generations could use to solve their problems. Dr. Robert Rosenthal builds on the paradox he sees in the Exodus:

> From the high ground of the Promised Land, we can at last look back over the terrain we've traveled and survey the journey in its entirety. When we do, we come upon an astonishing discovery. We see that there really was no journey. It didn't exist. What we experienced were but the different steps in awakening to the reality of Spirit—like successive veils of illusion lifted from before our eyes until at last we beheld the truth. . . . If we accept that Exodus is a parable, a teaching tale, then the Hebrews *cannot* reach the Promised Land, because we haven't reached it either. Their story is our story. It's incomplete, and necessarily so. And it

can only be completed by each of us making the journey and seeking to live life in full connection with Spirit.[23]

Today, followers of the Abrahamic religions try to glean moral and psychological lessons from the Exodus and apply them to their lives: liberation, faith, courage, revelation, fear, betrayal, murmuring, rebellion, repentance, renewal, battle, and eventual success. The Exodus is both a historic event and an archetypal event with endless allegoric applications. The whole Torah is about an ancient people and also about every person at all times. We gain insight into our own lives by studying the journeys of our ancestors and considering how they apply to our lives. The characters in the Bible are still alive in a spiritual sense, reaching out from ancient scrolls and showing us the way toward holiness, warning us of stumbling blocks along the way. Rabbi Irving Greenberg teaches:

> The Exodus is not a one-time event but a norm by which all of life should be judged and guided. The Exodus is an "orienting event"—an event that sets in motion and guides the Jewish way (and, ultimately, humanity's way) toward the Promised Land—an earth set free and perfected. And as they walk through local cultures and historical epochs, people can gauge whether they have lost the way to freedom by charting their behavior along the path against the Exodus norms.[24]

Modern psychologists have charted models of human development that can shed light on the maturation of a family, government, culture, or religion. Here are three.

Erik Erikson's Developmental Model

A highly respected and widely used model created by twentieth-century American psychologist Erik Erikson divides behavior into various stages of a person's life: infant, toddler, preschooler, school-age child, adolescent, young adult, middle-age adult, and older adult. As in an individual's life, a number of elements were at work simultaneously in the development of the Hebrews.

At the start of the forty years of the Exodus, they are liberated slaves at the stage of national infancy. In the wilderness, they progress through the early stages of development until they reach their young adult stage when they settle in Canaan. This is not a neat pattern of steady growth. As with individuals, a number of organic elements are at work simultaneously in their growth and development.

Middle-aged adult and older adult stages would not be reached until the Israelites established a stable kingdom with the construction of Solomon's temple. After the temple is destroyed by the Romans in 70 CE, a national reset takes place. The priestly era of the Israelites is over. By the beginning of the second century, the Jewish civilization has started over in a new infant stage with the birth of what is called Rabbinic Judaism. Christianity is born at this moment in history as well. Maybe today both Judaism and Christianity are in the older adult stage of national development.

Carl Jung's Developmental Model

Renowned twentieth-century psychologist Dr. Carl Jung employed the metaphor of morning, daytime, and nighttime to understand the personal development that occurs over a lifetime. Morning is equivalent to childhood and adolescence. Daytime is young adulthood through midlife. The evening of life is a person's elder years. Allegorically, we can understand the forty-year Exodus as if it were a lifetime.

Morning begins with the awakening—when the people heed God's call to prepare to be set free from enslavement. At dawn, the morning after the Passover, Moses leads the people out of Egypt to begin their first journey on the Exodus. In the wilderness, they are like children, dependent on God's mercy for food, water, and shelter, and struggle with the responsibilities that come with freedom.

The daytime of the Exodus begins when the younger generation realizes the older generation will not make it into the Promised Land with them. The team of Moses, Miriam, and Aaron teach the people how to integrate economic, governmental, and ethical wisdom into their religious lives. But it is Joshua who prepares the Israelites for battle, recognizing that they might have to fight to be able to return to Canaan, to take their place as adults in their own history.

Jung speaks of the evening of life as the descent into full maturity, coming off the mountains of our youth and into contact with the inner Self. In the Exodus story, this stage is represented by the deaths of Aaron, Miriam, and Moses, and the settlement of Canaan. In Jewish terms, what Jung called the Self with a capital S represents the realization that the soul is a spark of God. In the evening of life, the dichotomy between spirituality and physicality lessens, and the spiritual world is experienced as infusing the material world with sacred character. It is at this point, having completed a full developmental cycle, that the Hebrews are ready to become a nation.

Before the Hebrews cross the Jordan River, they camp at the mountains of *Abarim*. The name of this near-final camp comes from the same root as *Ivrim*, the name of the Hebrew people which, as already noted, means "people from the other side." After forty years, the people are ready to cross over from the other side—cross the Jordan River, cross over the fears of their parents—and no longer be strangers "from the other side" but be home as Israelites. This near-final camp is where the nation completes the process Jung calls individuation—integration of the individual to the Self. The people are ready to cross over into maturity, ready to fulfill the *mitzvot* they received forty years earlier at Sinai.

Gerald Heard's Five Ages of Man

In the 1960s, British historian Gerald Heard published his psychology of human history, *The Five Ages of Man*. This model can be applied both to individuals and to the development of the Jewish people. Rabbi Zalman Schachter-Shalomi summarizes Heard's stages as:

1. Pre-Individual: one with nature and tribe—no real sense of individuality
2. Proto-Individual: rebellious heroic period—becoming an individual
3. Ascetic Era: mid-individual era—self-improvement, desire to transcend
4. Humanic Era: renaissance—focus on physical world, improve social order
5. Post-Individual: second maturity—highest potential[25]

As slaves in Egypt, the Hebrews are Pre-Individuals with a weak sense of individuality due to the subjugation of enslavement. Jewish tradition doesn't name individuals who stood out for heroic activity in the first centuries of captivity. The heroic stories of the Proto-Individual stage begin with the birth of Moses and the heroic women Miriam, Batya, Shiphrah, and Puah. During this period Moses struggles with his stepbrother, Rameses II, to liberate the slaves.

The book of Numbers offers stories at the height of the Proto-Individual stage—heroes (Joshua, Miriam, Aaron), rebels (Dathan, Korach, Abiram), and enemies (Amalek, Baalam, Balak). After twenty years in the wilderness, and as the older generation is dying, the younger generation begins to take leadership. At this point, they begin to enter an Ascetic Era with a focus on the future and self-improvement. The book of Leviticus fits the bill for the Ascetic stage, with its focus on morality, transcendence, and holiness.

After being forged as a new nation in the wilderness, when they settle in Canaan, the younger generation is ready to improve the social order. The Humanic Era begins and continues through the era of the Judges, Prophets, and Kings. The Post-Individual Age cannot begin until the Israelites establish unity between the kingdoms of Judea in the south and Israel in the north. This is the era of the later prophets Ezra and Nehemiah, the canonization of the Tanakh, and planting of the seeds of what would later become Rabbinic Judaism.

With the destruction of the Second Temple in 70 CE, the cycle of Heard's five ages starts all over again with the birth of post-Temple Judaism. Hopefully, we are again in a Post-Individual age—in what Jews and Christians call the Messianic Era, an age of peace where swords will be turned into plowshares. The prelude to this period is known as the "birth pangs of the Messiah," an era that ultimately leads to worldwide harmony and peace. As Jesus said, "all this is but the beginning of the birth pangs" (Matt. 24:8). We can only hope that amidst all the bad news we hear today, there is also emerging the birth of a new consciousness of our mutual interdependence with each other and with our planet. Just as the Exodus began with the catastrophe of enslavement but led to a great redemption, so we pray to God that the catastrophes of our own era are merely preludes to an even greater redemption and the liberation of all humanity as well as the planet.

PART TWO

Reimagining Exodus

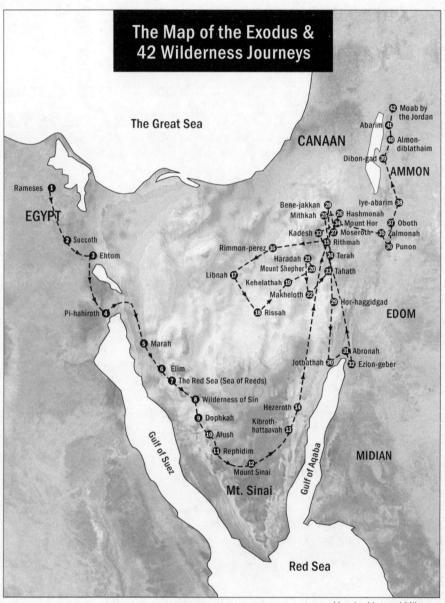

The Map of the Exodus & 42 Wilderness Journeys

The Great Sea

CANAAN

42 Moab by the Jordan

Abarim 41

40 Almond-diblathaim

Dibon-gad 39

AMMON

Rameses 1

EGYPT

2 Succoth

3 Ehtom

Pi-hahiroth 4

5 Marah

6 Elim

7 The Red Sea (Sea of Reeds)

8 Wilderness of Sin

9 Dophkah

10 Alush

11 Rephidim

12 Mount Sinai

Mt. Sinai

Gulf of Suez

Iye-abarim 35

Bene-jakkan 28

Mithkah 25 26 Hashmonah

34 Mount Hor 37 Oboth

Moseroth

Kadesh 33 27 35 Zalmonah

15 Rithmah 36 Punon

Rimmon-perez 16

Haradah 21

Mount Shepher 20

Libnah 17

Kehelathah 19 23 Tahath

24 Terah

Makheloth 22

18 Rissah

29 Hor-haggidgad

EDOM

31 Abronah

Jotbathah 30 32 Ezion-geber

Hezeroth 14

Kibroth-hattaavah 13

Gulf of Aqaba

MIDIAN

Red Sea

Map by Howard Milgram

Timeline of the 42 Journeys of the Exodus[26]

Year after Exodus	Journey #	Name of Camp	Commentary
Year 1	1	*Rameses*	There were 11 journeys from the start of the Exodus in *Rameses* to the revelation of the Torah at Mount Sinai 50 days later. Sinai was the twelfth camp for the Israelites.
	2	*Succoth*	
	3	*Ehtom*	
	4	*Pi-hahiroth*	
	5	*Marah*	
	6	*Elim*	
	7	*The Red Sea (Sea of Reeds)*	
	8	*Wilderness of Sin*	God wanted the Hebrews to enter the Promised Land early in the Exodus. In year 2 at *Ritmah*, the scouts expressed their fear of entering Canaan. This led to the exile of the Israelites in the wilderness for a total of 40 years.
	9	*Dophkah*	
	10	*Alush*	
	11	*Rephidim*	
	12	*Mount Sinai*	
Year 2	13	*Kibroth-hattaavah*	Rabbi Aryeh Kaplan reports that some scholars say the Israelites lived in *Ritmah* for 19 years, and that Ibn Ezra suggested that it was in *Kadesh* that they lived for 19 years.
	14	*Hezeroth*	
	15	*Rithmah*	

	16	*Rimmon-perez*	The popular image of the Israelites wandering in the wilderness for 40 years is incorrect. Rather, the Hebrews were mostly settled, staying in individual campsites for long periods.
	17	*Libnah*	
	18	*Rissah*	
	19	*Kehelathah*	
	20	*Mount Shepher*	
	21	*Haradah*	
Years 3–19	22	*Makheloth*	Whether the Israelites settled in *Rithmah* or *Kadesh* for 19 years, they would have lived in the other camps for approximately one year each. The first and the fortieth year they camped for approximately one month at each campsite.
	23	*Tahath*	
	24	*Terah*	
	25	*Mithkah*	
	26	*Hashmonah*	
	27	*Moseroth*	
	28	*Bene-jakkan*	
	29	*Hor-haggidgad*	Rather than wandering aimlessly, the Israelites were journeying and trying to avoid warfare with local tribes.
	30	*Jotbathah*	
	31	*Abronah*	
	32	*Ezion-geber*	
Years 20–39	33	*Kadesh*	According to Ibn Ezra, the Israelites lived in the *Wilderness of Zin* at *Kadesh* for 19 years.
Year 40	34	*Mount Hor*	There were 9 camps in the fortieth year after the Exodus. *The Plains of Moab* was the final camp and staging ground before the Israelites entered the Promised Land at Jericho under the leadership of Joshua.
	35	*Zalmonah*	
	36	*Punon*	
	37	*Oboth*	
	38	*Iye-abarim*	
	39	*Dibon-gad*	
	40	*Almon-diblathaim*	
	41	*Abarim*	
	42	*Moab by the Jordan*	

Forty-Two Journeys and Campsites—
Numbers 33:1–49

200 miles from Egypt to Israel
Numbers 33:1

*These are the stages by which the Israelites went out of the land of Egypt
in military formation under the leadership of Moses and Aaron.*

Although it's less than 200 miles from the Suez in Egypt to Israel, it took Moses and the Israelites forty years to get there. The number forty is a familiar and ubiquitous symbol in Jewish and Christian traditions: Noah stays on the ark forty days after the flood; Moses is at Sinai for forty days; King Solomon rules for forty years; and so on. In the Younger Testament, Jesus spends forty days in the wilderness tempted by Satan, and we count another forty days between the Resurrection and the Ascension. Similarly, the Exodus journey of the Israelites lasts for forty years. In both Judaism and Christianity, forty is understood metaphorically as a complete period for transition—possibly biologically rooted in the forty weeks of human pregnancy.

Numbers 33:1–49 is little more than a listing of the forty-two places where the children of Israel camped. What was the intent of naming them without explanation? Rabbi Joseph Hertz, former chief rabbi of the British Empire, says this chapter "was written to serve as a memorial not only of historical interest but of deep religious significance. Every journey and every halting-place had its suggestion for the instruction, admonition, or encouragement of Israel."[27]

The Baal Shem Tov, one of Judaism's most important teachers, suggests that this unusually long list of place names is actually a psychological map of the ups and downs in a lifetime. He teaches that each of us relives the forty-two journeys and resting places during our lives. Rabbi Menachem Mendel Schneerson proposes that the journeys are comparable to the journey of a soul from the spiritual world to the physical world: "This entire sequence is intended to be a continuing progression toward spiritual growth. Even those stages in the journey of the Jewish people which are connected with negative occurrences have a positive impetus at their source."[28]

The names of these places are transliterated in English Bibles, so they read as an indecipherable jumble of sounds from the Egyptian or Hebrew. We can make educated guesses based on what Torah describes in particular locales and the word origins of the names. Some would have been Egyptian sites familiar to Israelites in that era; a few might have been named by the Semitic Hyksos who lived in the Sinai as shepherds. But a great many of the residential camps were likely named by the Hebrews during their sojourn back to Canaan. When we look at the root meanings of these place names together, a magnificent series of metaphors emerges that can serve as a template for understanding the complexity and challenges of our own personal journeys. Rabbi Lawrence Hoffman writes, "Music consists of notes, but also rests. So, too, journeys are as much about pausing as journeying. . . . Stops are opportunities for correction. . . . Do we properly use each stop to correct our course before starting up again?"[29]

The Israelites dwelt in each campsite for an average of a year. (See Timeline of the 42 Journeys on pages 38–39.) Eleventh-century Torah commentator Rashi teaches that except for the first and final year of the Exodus, the Hebrews journeyed only twenty-eight times in thirty-eight years. The campsite names designated geographical features of the location, while also mirroring the experiences of the people, both positive and negative. The chart of campsite names is a speculative peek at what the people intended in naming the places. (See Metaphorical Translations of the 42 Journeys on pages 46–48.[30])

We can apply the names allegorically to all journeys: collective journeys of a culture as well as personal journeys. To make the Exodus relevant and immediate, we can imagine each journey as a spiritual expedition out of our own "inner Egypt"—a restriction or narrow place that holds us from our personal "Promised Land." Dr. Mary Ellen Chase speaks of the universal application of these and other biblical journeys:

> In the Old Testament . . . all wayfaring takes upon itself, through the associative power of the Hebrew imagination, the impression of a search or a quest. Also, through his singular emotional power of identification, the Hebrew writer can throw over and around these journeys the equally strong impression that they are not peculiar to one people at one time, but are instead the ageless experiences of all.[31]

At one site during the Exodus, the newly emancipated slaves experience exaltation and hope, while at another they are consumed with fear and doubt. This emotional drama is reflected in many of names of the campsites. Cantor Gershon Silins suggests that all of these place names and their significance would have been well known to the Israelites of that time:

> Narratives and lists are metaphors. They serve as one way human beings communicate with one another about things worth remembering and the thoughts associated with them. . . . We can imagine that since the list is just a list, our ancestors heard it and knew exactly what these places represented. They had complete stories in mind, having full understanding of the events that took place there (as we do when we hear the words Watergate or Woodstock, for example). They probably thought those stories would always be remembered by the hearers of the list. So one thing we learn is that even the most important story may be forgotten if the hearers do not pass it on. What happened at *Ritmah* or at *Rimmon-perez*? We will never know.[32]

Following are interpretations drawn from the etymological roots of just a few of the encampment names listed in Numbers 33:1–49.

Rameses to Succoth
Numbers 33:5

The Israelites set out from Rameses, and camped at Succoth.

After liberation, the Hebrews used the Egyptian city of Rameses, named for a previous pharaoh of Egypt, as their staging area to prepare to go into the Sinai Peninsula. The name of this city, roughly translated "born of the sun" (*Ra-meses*), means "son of the sun god Ra." From there they went to Succoth, a place the Hebrews probably named, usually translated as "booths." The modern English word *booth* connotes a temporary tent at a marketplace. In Hebrew, though, it means "temporary huts" or shelters. Succoth is also the name of the Jewish autumn harvest festival—the original Thanksgiving. At the start of the festival families build succoth where they gather, eat, pray, give, sing, tell stories, and give thanks during the weeklong holiday. Hence, in the etymological translation chart, Numbers 33:5 is interpreted as "they set out from 'Born of the Sun' and camped at 'Thanksgiving Harvest Shelters'."

Pi-hahiroth to Marah
Numbers 33:8

They set out from Pi-hahiroth...and camped at Marah.

Pi-hahiroth is one of the campsites with an existing Egyptian name, and the original meaning is uncertain. Nevertheless, the Midrash renders *Pi-hahiroth* into Hebrew as "mouth of freedom," which of course mirrors the experience of the newly liberated slaves—freedom! The next campsite is Marah. The Torah reports, "When they came to Marah, they could not drink the water of Marah because it was bitter. That is why it was called Marah" (Exod. 15:23). Clearly anyone camping at a bitter stream might name the place Bitter, but the Torah also describes the complaining of the people. The name, then, describes not only the bitter water, but also the bitter state of the Israelites. Hence, they set out from the "Mouth of Freedom" and camped at "Bitter Waters."

Sinai to Kibroth-hattaavah
Numbers 33:16

They set out from the wilderness of Sinai and camped at Kibroth-hattaavah.

In Numbers 33:16 we get only the name of the campsite: Kibroth-hattaavah. However, in an earlier verse (Num. 11:34), the Torah tells us the meaning: "So that place was called Kibroth-hattaavah, because there they buried the people who had the craving." The name literally means "Graves of Craving." A year earlier, the Hebrews had received the Ten Commandments at Mount Sinai, and remained in the area. Since Mount Sinai was the place of the most profound theophany and national revelation recorded in history, I translate it as "Place of Revelation." In the etymological translation chart I translated the verse as "they set out from 'Place of Revelation' and camped at 'Graves of Craving.'"

Terah to Mithkah
Numbers 33:28

They set out from Terah and camped at Mithkah.

Terah in Hebrew is spelled the same way as the name of Abraham's father (Gen. 11:25). The etymology of this word is uncertain, but it might mean "wanderer" or "wild goat." Was this site named as a memorial for one of the Hebrew ancestors, Abraham's father, or was it a description of how the people felt—like wandering wild goats? *Mithkah* in Hebrew means "sweetness." According to the *Targum Yonaton* (a first-century BCE Aramaic translation), sweet, fresh water was found here. I translate it as "they set out from 'Remembering Abraham's Father' and camped at 'Sweetness'."

—

Do the forty-two place names form a logical developmental structure or a random list of encampments? It is almost certain that the Hebrews were not consciously creating a pattern. People are rarely self-aware of the degree to which they are making history. That's the job of hindsight. The chart of etymological translations is intended to be poetic and not to confirm a logical pattern. Nevertheless, it's a joy to look into the poetry of the names and imagine what the children of Israel might have been experiencing at each campsite. Translating from any language offers the translator a range of interpretive possibilities, and the Hebrew roots of the campsite names offer a range of meanings—I chose one of many possible interpretations for each site. Other Hebrew readers will prefer different interpretive translations.

Read the chart of metaphorical translations as a poem—not as untrue, but as a different kind of truth. The Pentateuch was never intended to be a history text only. Rather, it is a guide for life, a template to place upon our own lives, a mirror in which we can see our own reflections and see how we are all created *b'tzelem Eloheem; imago dei* in Latin; in the image of God. It is fascinating to take the actual and speculative origins of the place names in Numbers 33:1–49 and string them together as if they were some hidden message that has traveled across the ocean of time, preserved like a message in a bottle washed up on shore and waiting for us to find it.

Metaphorical Translations of the 42 Journeys Listed in Numbers 33:3–49

Based on the etymology of place names

Translated by Rabbi David Zaslow

Camp Names	Metaphorical Translation
1) They set out from Rameses and camped at Succoth.	They set out from "Born of the Sun" and camped at "Thanksgiving Harvest Shelters."
2) They set out from Succoth and camped at Etham.	They set out from "Thanksgiving Harvest Shelters" and camped at "Fortress-by-the-Sea."
3) They set out from Etham and camped at Pi-hahiroth.	They set out from "Fortress-by-the-Sea" and camped at "Mouth of Freedom."
4) They set out from Pi-hahiroth and camped at Marah.	They set out from "Mouth of Freedom" and camped at "Bitter Waters."
5) They set out from Marah and camped at Elim.	They set out from "Bitter Waters" and camped at "Strong Trees and Rams."
6) They set out from Elim and camped at the Red Sea.	They set out from "Strong Trees and Rams" and camped at the "Reed Sea."
7) They set out from the Red Sea and camped at Sin.	They set out from the "Reed Sea" and camped at "Where the Moon Was Worshipped."
8) They set out from Sin and camped at Dophkah.	They set out from "Where the Moon Was Worshipped" and camped at "Knocking-Pulse"
9) They set out from Dophkah and camped at Alush.	They set out from "Knocking-Pulse" and camped at "I Will Knead Bread."
10) They set out from Alush and camped at Rephidim.	They set out from "I Will Knead Bread" and camped at "Rest Our Weakened Hands."
11) They set out from Rephidim and camped at Mt. Sinai.	They set out from "Rest Our Weakened Hands" and camped at "Place of Revelation."
12) They set out from Mt. Sinai and camped at Kibroth-hattaavah.	They set out from "Place of Revelation" and camped at "Graves of Craving."

13) They set out from Kibroth-hattaavah and camped at Hezeroth.	They set out from "Graves of Craving" and camped at "Settled Abode."
14) They set out from Hezeroth and camped at Rithmah.	They set out from "Settled Abode" and camped at "Wild Broom Juniper."
15) They set out from Rithmah and camped at Rimmon-perez.	They set out from "Wild Broom Juniper" and camped at "Bursting Pomegranate."
16) They set out from Rimmon-perez and camped at Libnah.	They set out from "Bursting Pomegranate" and camped at "Moon White Bricks."
17) They set out from Libnah and camped at Rissah.	They set out from "Moon White Bricks" and camped at "Dew Drop Ruins."
18) They set out from Rissah and camped at Kehelathah.	They set out from "Dew Drop Ruins" and camped at "Being in Community."
19) They set out from Kehelathah and camped at Mt. Shepher.	They set out from "Being in Community" and camped at "Illuminated Beauty."
20) They set out from Mt. Shepher and camped at Haradah.	They set out from "Illuminated Beauty" and camped at the "Shaking in Fear."
21) They set out from Haradah and camped at Makheloth.	They set out from "Shaking in Fear" and camped at "Assembly of Voices."
22) They set out from Makheloth and camped at Tahath.	They set out from "Assembly of Voices" and camped at "Beneath and Under."
23) They set out from Tahath and camped at Terah.	They set out from "Beneath and Under" and camped at "Remembering Abraham's Father."
24) They set out from Terah and camped at Mithkah.	They set out from "Remembering Abraham's Father" and camped at "Sweetness."
25) They set out from Mithkah and camped at Hashmonah.	They set out from "Sweetness" and camped at "Oil of Eight."
26) They set out from Hashmonah and camped at Moseroth.	They set out from "Oil of Eight" and camped at "Bonds of Ethics."
27) They set out from Moseroth and camped at Bene-jakkan.	They set out from "Bonds of Ethics" and camped at "Wells of the Sons of Twisting."

28) They set out from Bene-jakkan and camped at Hor-haggidgad.	They set out from "Wells of the Sons of Twisting" and camped at "Inroad Hole."
29) They set out from Hor-haggidgad and camped at Jotbathah.	They set out from "Inroad Hole" and camped at "Goodness."
30) They set out from Jotbathah and camped at Abronah.	They set out from "Goodness" and camped at "Passage Over."
31) They set out from Abronah and camped at Ezion-geber.	They set out from "Passage Over" and camped at "Giant's Backbone."
32) They set out from Ezion-geber and camped at Kadesh.	They set out from "Giant's Backbone" and camped at "A Holy Place."
33) They set out from Kadesh and camped at Mt. Hor.	They set out from "A Holy Place" and camped at "Mountain on a Mountain."
34) They set from Mt. Hor and camped at Zalmonah.	They set out from "Mountain on a Mountain" and camped at "Shady Image Place."
35) They set out from Zalmonah and camped at Punon.	They set out from "Shady Image Place" and camped at "Obscurity in Darkness."
36) They set out from Punon and camped at Oboth.	They set out from "Obscurity in Darkness" and camped at "Bottle Rattling Ghosts."
37) They set out from Oboth and camped at Iye-abarim.	They set out from "Bottle Rattling Ghosts" and camped at "The Ruins of Passing Over."
38) They set out from Iye-abarim and camped at Dibon-gad.	They set out from "The Ruins of Passing Over" and camped at "Waste and Fortune."
39) They set out from Dibon-gad and camped at Almon-diblathaim.	They set out from "Waste and Fortune" and camped at "Secret of Two Fig Cakes."
40) They set out from Almon-diblathaim and camped at Abarim.	They set out from "Secret of Two Fig Cakes" and camped at "Mountains of Crossing Over."
41) They set out from Abarim and camped at Plains of Moab.	They set out from "Mountains of Crossing Over" and camped at the "Plains of a Fathers Seed."
42) They set out from Plains of Moab and camped by the Jordan.	They set out from "Plains of a Father's Seed" and camped at "Ready to Cross the River."

Shiphrah and Puah: Brightness and Brilliancy—Exodus 1:15–16

The king of Egypt said to the Hebrew midwives,
one of whom was named Shiphrah and the other Puah.

What we call the book of Exodus is actually called the book of *Shemot*, Hebrew for "Names," because of its opening line: "These are the *names* of the sons of Israel who came to Egypt" (Exod. 1:1). The verses that follow list the names of the sons of Jacob who came to Egypt hundreds of years before the enslavement of their descendants. It's a mystery that even though it is called the book of Names, many of the characters in the opening chapters go unnamed.

The pharaoh who rules over Egypt is unnamed (Exod. 1:8). The father and mother of Moses, although we are told they are from the tribe of Levi, are unnamed (Exod. 2:1) until later in Exodus (6:20). Pharaoh's daughter, the princess of Egypt who rescues and adopts the as-yet-unnamed baby in the basket, is unnamed (Exod. 2:5). And Moses's big sister, who guards the basket with the baby until it is discovered (Exod. 2:4), goes unnamed until much later. Only the midwives Shiphrah and Puah are named (Exod. 1:15). Eventually, Pharaoh's daughter (who remains unnamed through the entire Pentateuch) names the baby: "She named him Moses, 'because,' she said, 'I drew him out of the water'" (Exod. 2:10).

Who are these midwives, and why do they, along with Moses, get named? Maybe the answer is in the meaning of their names. *Shiphrah* comes from a root meaning "brightness" and *Puah* is derived from a root meaning "brilliancy" or "splendid." Both names have to do with light, and only light can make things seen. The role of midwives is to bring new life from the darkness of the womb into the world. When Moses is drawn from the water by Pharaoh's daughter, it is a kind of rebirth—an already "living" soul is ready to take on a physical form. Moses is brought into the light of the world and can then receive a name. The other characters will remain hidden in the shadows for a while.

The contemporary expression "being in the dark" implies a lack of knowledge. In Hebrew Scripture, however, that darkness does not imply that something is missing or wrong. Rather, it implies something is hidden. In the first day of creation, darkness is preexistent—it is not something that God has to create like light. Darkness seems to be the necessary precondition, the canvas onto which the creation takes place. Without darkness, there are can be no light. So it is at the beginning of Exodus/Shemot: the names of key characters will remain hidden.

We learn Moses's sister's name, Miriam, eighty years later, after the crossing of the Red Sea. The rabbis give the pharaoh's daughter a name much later in Jewish history: Batya, which means "daughter of God."[33] In the magnificent literature of the Tanakh, as in all great stories, there is a plot device called "the reveal." Something is only revealed, brought into the light, at the exact moment it will have the most impact. By not telling the reader certain names, a curiosity and desire to learn more is aroused.

For example, in the book of Esther, we learn that Esther's identity as a Jew must remain hidden until the right time. Moments before the villain Haman is to murder all the Jews, Esther reveals herself and saves her people. When the Persian name Esther is rendered into Hebrew it actually means "hidden." God is also hidden in the book of Esther. It and the Song of Solomon are the only books in the Bible where God is hidden and not directly named.

God is also hidden in the first part of the book of Exodus. Not until forty years after "Brightness" and "Brilliancy" (Shiphrah and Puah) drew Moses from the womb, and Pharaoh's daughter drew Moses from the basket, do we find out God's most hidden name. Not until the burning bush does God tell Moses the divine name to use when he comes to deliver the people from bondage: *Eheyeh Asher Eheyeh*, I Will Be What I Will Be. Just as Moses and the tribes of Israel began to despair that they would never again see the light, the Light is revealed.

The Bush Was Not Consumed—
Exodus 3:2–3

There the angel of the LORD appeared to him in a flame of fire out of a bush;
he looked, and the bush was blazing, yet it was not consumed.
Then Moses said, "I must turn aside and look at this great sight,
and see why the bush is not burned up."

A bush on fire but not consumed. Was this a miraculous sight? Or a common sight that Moses had just not noticed before? My friend Dr. Howard Morningstar suggests that all plants are actually on fire but not consumed since they absorb the "fire" from the sun during photosynthesis to create sugar—the universal fuel of life. "Fire green as grass," Dylan Thomas said.

The Baal Shem Tov (eighteenth-century Rabbi Israel ben Eliezer) explained the difference between nature and a miracle. The first time a person sees something it's called a miracle. The second time it's called nature. The biblical era drew fewer lines between the natural and the spiritual worlds. The sudden appearance of "the angel of the LORD" in a flame might have appeared "great" and mysterious to him but not unnatural.

Theologians describe Moses's encounter at the burning bush as a theophany, a personal encounter with an appearance of the divine. This miraculous event was certainly a turning point in Moses's life. Jungian psychologist Dr. Edward Edinger proposes that it "is a classic image of an encounter with the Self. . . . Fire is a frequent synonym for the divine. . . . The unconsuming nature of the fire emphasizes its transpersonal nature. It is desire that is not quenched by personal satisfactions, the desire Jung speaks of as 'a thirsting for the eternal.'"[34]

So, was Moses's encounter with the burning bush a manifestation of psychological transformation, or truly an encounter with God? Perhaps it was both. He met God *and* a part of himself. Dr. David Gelernter insightfully points out the intersection between the theophany and Moses's psychological state:

> "I have seen, yes *seen*, the affliction of my people in Egypt, and I have heard their screams in the face of their taskmasters; I do know their sufferings." These words seem to fit Moses' emotional and cognitive state perfectly; but they are spoken by the Lord. At the bush, then, Moses hears what is on his own mind; in listening to the Lord he listens, as it were, to his own mind speaking. He is forced to confront not only the Lord but his own dangerous, difficult, heroic desire to return to Egypt and lead his people out of slavery. . . . That the bush is on fire but not consumed reminds us that Moses will die in old age with "his eyes undimmed and his powers unabated." But the image also seems to tell him that he will burn with passion his whole life and never be done burning; he will never cool down, cool off, come to rest.[35]

Moses's personal, fiery encounter with God at the bush seems to foreshadow the communal fiery encounter at Sinai. As mentioned earlier, the Hebrew word for bush, *sneh*, has the same root as Sinai—named because the mountain had so many thorny bushes. Both theophanies—at the burning bush and Mount Sinai—are archetypical events representing revelatory moments every person experiences. The bush is personal revelation; Sinai in a communal or group setting. Later, Christianity would also adopt the concept of revelation through fire in the Pentecost. In the noncanonical Gospel of Thomas, Jesus says, "He who is near me is near the fire."[36]

Moses was not so much in an altered state of consciousness as in a hyperconscious state when he encountered the bush. Maybe people today are in an "altered" state when, surrounded by the miracle of nature, they fail to see the bushes unconsumed by fire. The role of all our religions is to bring the faithful back, back to the place where heaven meets earth, where the world of the miraculous meets the world of nature, where our psyches meet our souls, where God is encountered in a bush that is not consumed.

Moses, Moses! Here I Am.—Exodus 3:4

When the LORD saw that he had turned aside to see,
God called to him out of the bush, "Moses, Moses!"
And he said, "Here I am."

God calls Moses by name from the burning bush, not once but twice: "Moses, Moses!" When calling to Abraham, Jacob, and Samuel, three of the most important figures in the Elder Testament,* God did the same. Why twice? This same pattern is used in the Younger Testament when Jesus calls out *Saul, Saul; Simon, Simon; Martha, Martha;* and even *My God My God* as he was drawing his final breaths.

In Hebrew, doubles are used—such as Song of Songs, Holy of Holies, servant of servants—to point to the superlative, the ultimate of something. Often when you see the word *surely* in an English translation of the Hebrew Bible, it is actually one of these double words. When Jethro is advising his son-in-law Moses about delegating responsibility, in English it is rendered, "You will *surely* wear yourself out, both you and these people with you" (Exod. 18:18). The word *surely* is not there in the Hebrew; it is the word "wear" doubled to add power to Jethro's sage advice.

When Moses hears his name "Moses, Moses!" at the burning bush, he instantly pays heed. God could have been saying, "Moses, yes you, Moses"—or "Moses, now really pay attention to this, Moses"—or even, "I, God, call your name two times—first to the aspect of Moses that lives in the natural world, and second to the aspect of Moses that lives in the spiritual world. Moses, Moses!" Two parts of the same person!

When Moses hears the Holy One call, he responds by uttering a fantastic biblical word: *hineni*. When referring to a person, *hineni* means

---

* I call the Old Testament and New Testament the Elder Testament and Younger Testament. See my explanation in the Introduction on page xx.

"behold," or "here I am." When responding to God, the word has the additional meaning of "I am ready." Not just the "here I am" when a friend asks, "Where are you?" The biblical *hineni* is a profound response to being called: here I am, right here, fully here, fully ready for whatever God or someone might ask of me.

We can discern a behavioral response pattern at the bush. First, Moses can see the angel who appears to him as if to say, "See this." Moses turns and sees. When God "sees" that Moses turns to see the bush, we then hear the call: "Moses, Moses!" A version of the verb *see* is used five times in three verses. With no pause whatsoever, Moses responds, "*Hineni*"—"Here I am, fully ready!" Here is the pattern of Moses's actions: he looks, he beholds, he turns, he listens, he is ready.

In our lives sometimes our *hineni* response mechanism to God's call is operational, sometimes not. When we hear the divine call there isn't time to say, "Let me think about this," or "I'd better check my calendar." When God calls once, we're ready or we're not. But if God calls our name twice, meaning we are needed for the Ultimate Plan, God *sees* that we are ready to *see* the Plan and that we have the adequate faith to say, "My God, My God, *hineni*, I am ready."

What's Your Name?—Exodus 3:13–14

Moses said to God, "If I come to the Israelites and say to them,
'The God of your ancestors has sent me to you,'
and they ask me, 'What is his name?' what shall I say to them?"
God said to Moses, "I AM WHO I AM."

How can God have a name? A name is by its nature a limitation. If I am David, then I am not Ari or Samuel. In other words, my name limits me to being David and not people by a thousand other names. Once we give God a name, we are limiting God—we are making finite that which is infinite. Our Hebrew ancestors realized the theological dilemma of naming God and preferred using titles and attributes, both masculine and feminine, plural and singular, to *name* the divine.

Just by naming God we are faced with this contradiction: if I name that which is infinite and eternal, I am limiting that which is unlimited; if I do not name God, how can I have a personal relationship with the divine? I remember an incident with my teacher Reb Zalman. In answering a question from a student, he gave two opposite responses and the student pointed this out. Reb Zalman offered a vignette from David Slabotsky:

> Rabbi Ishmael, when he taught at Safed, related to his pupils the many true and holy names of God, as well as the basic principle that God could never be named. Hearing this, one of Rabbi Ishmael's pupils stood up and addressed his teacher: "Rabbi, in what you have just said there is a contradiction." "Yes," Rabbi Ishmael replied, "but only a contradiction."[37]

The word *contradiction* comes from two Latin roots: *contra* meaning against and *dicere* meaning speak. A contradiction is just something that we can't speak about simply—that doesn't mean on a deeper level it cannot be true, or partially true. In Reb Zalman's words:

> Contradictions we can live with. Nothing we can say about God can survive the rigors of logical analysis. But that shouldn't get in the way of our search for the presence we have felt in our most spiritually open—or spiritually hungry—moments. If there is a tension between what we know in our minds and what we feel in our hearts, then let's stay with that tension. If there is a contradiction, let us take it upon ourselves.[38]

God in the Hebrew Bible is Father, King, Beloved, Lord, Merciful One, Highest One, Savior, Creator, Shepherd. And then there are the compound titles: Lord of Hosts, Ruler of the Universe, Redeemer of Israel, Former of Light, God the Most High. In the Tanakh, Talmud, and prayer book, there are dozens of primary titles of God and dozens of compound titles.

But at the time Moses encountered God at the burning bush, the Tanakh had not yet been written, much less the prayer book or Talmud, so he did not have this list of names. Traditional Jewish commentary teaches that Moses lived in Egypt until he was forty years old, when he fled in exile to Midian. He then lived with his father-in-law, Jethro, until he was eighty. Although he believed in a single God, he was still attached to the idea prevalent in North Africa and the Middle East that all gods have specific names. So, when Moses asks God for a name at the burning bush, the Midrash tells us that God responded in this way:

> God said to Moses, "You want to know My Name? Well, I am called according to My work. When I am judging created beings, I am called Elohim (God). When I suspend judgement I am called el Shaddai (God Almighty). When I am merciful

toward my world, I am called YHJVH, which refers to the attribute of Mercy. Thus ehyeh asher ehyeh [see below] in virtue of my deeds."[39]

The Hebrews had been living among the Egyptians who had specific names for all the gods, and Moses understood that the Hebrews would want to know the name of the deity that was about to free them. And so, Moses asks God what he should tell them. What does God say? In Hebrew the words are *Eheyeh Asher Eheyeh*, often translated as "I am who I am." A better translation is "I will be what I will be." God says to tell the Hebrews that the deity who will rescue them is not a local god who occupies a particular place, but the God of time itself, the God of becoming. The word *eheyeh*, while difficult to translate literally, is made of the letters that spell the words of being: was, is, and will be. "I will be what I will be," God tells Moses. "Tell that to the people."

God adds immediately, "Thus you shall say to the Israelites, 'The Lord, the God of your ancestors, the God of Abraham, the God of Isaac, and the God of Jacob, has sent me to you' (Exod. 3:14–15). God seems to modify the name he gives Moses by adding the title, "The Lord, the God of your ancestors." Wasn't *Eheyeh Asher Eheyeh* enough? Why did God have to add anything? The Midrash offers us an explanation. Moses, it says, tells God that having been enslaved for hundreds of years, the Hebrews could not comprehend the name "I will be what I will be." He argues that they need a concrete name. God concedes the point and adds, "The Lord, the God of your ancestors." Moses breathes a sigh of relief as if to say, "This name the people will understand!"

We tend to be enslaved to the idea that God should be—needs to be—logically consistent. Imagine how liberated we will be when we can accept that God exists not only throughout space, but also throughout all time—not only omnipotent and omniscient, but also omnipresent, the One who was, is, and will be.

Pharaoh's Heart Condition—Exodus 4:21

And the LORD said to Moses, "When you go back to Egypt,
see that you perform before Pharaoh all the wonders
that I have put in your power; but I will harden his heart,
so that he will not let the people go."

God commands Moses to tell Rameses II, "Let my people go,"
while at the same time telling Moses that Rameses will say
"no." The Holy One's words might have baffled Moses just as they have
readers of the Torah for millennia. If God hardened his heart, as the text
plainly says, then Pharaoh has no free will to choose right over wrong. If
Pharaoh has no free will, how can he be held responsible for not letting
the people go? It seems that when God hardens Pharaoh's heart, it is a
divine reaction to Pharaoh's own choice to be hard-hearted.

Yeshiva University professor Dr. David Shatz puts it this way:
"Hardening is God's way of respecting Pharaoh's own prior choices,
of helping him to follow in his previously freely chosen path while
imposing upon him full responsibility for those hardened acts. He has
the opportunity to act in accordance with his true self."[40] And why did
God tell Moses in advance that Pharaoh would say "no"? Rabbi Joseph
Hertz, Chief Rabbi of the United Kingdom in the early twentieth
century, offers this explanation:

> For God to make it impossible for a man to obey Him, and
> then punish him for his disobedience, would be both unjust
> and contrary to the fundamental Jewish belief in Freedom
> of the Will...every successive refusal on the part of Pharaoh
> to listen to the message of Moses froze up his better nature
> more and more, until it seemed as if God had hardened his
> heart. But this is only so because Pharaoh had first hardened
> it himself, and continued doing so. The Omniscient God

knew beforehand whither his obstinacy would lead Pharaoh, and prepared Moses for initial failure by warning him that Pharaoh's heart would become "hardened."[41]

The principle of free will applies to all of us when we do wrong. And when we make mistakes, as we will, the process of *teshuvah*, repentance, is always available. All energy to act comes from God, so we are left to ponder this paradox: if people can only do good, there is no free will. If they can choose to do wrong, the energy to do that harm is the same energy they could have used to do good.

Since Rameses exercises free will again and again for harm, what causes his change of heart? A hint at what might be going on is embedded in the three distinct Hebrew verbs that are all translated "hardened." If the ten plagues are stages leading to freedom, the different verbs for "hardened" may be catalysts to make the transformation possible. Pharaoh didn't have a sudden change; his heart was opened through a three-step process represented by the words *kashah*, "to be made hard"; *kaved*, "to be made heavy"; and *hazak*, "to be made strong."

1. Shaping—*kashah*, to be made hard, is related to a word meaning "hammered work," as in a piece of metal jewelry. It is an interesting irony that hammering actually softens metal so it can be shaped. So when God *kashahs* Pharaoh's heart, he is actually softening and preparing Pharaoh for personal transformation. As with jewelry, hammering implies shaping—this is the first stage in the transformation. How did God hammer at Pharaoh's heart? With plague after plague after plague.

2. Glorifying—*kaved*, to be made heavy, also means "honor" and "glory." In a Midrash, God says to Pharaoh, "With the same word with which you show yourself to be heavy-hearted (*kaved*) I will get honor (*kavod*) for Myself" (Genesis Rabbah

9:8). How did God get this honor into Pharaoh's heart? By showing him the miraculous exemption of the children of Israel from the plagues, and by limiting the scope and duration of the plagues affecting the Egyptians.

3. Strengthening—*Hazak*, to be made strong, by extension means "to give strength." Having been raised to believe he is the living embodiment of the sun god Ra, Pharaoh would need great strength and humility to acknowledge the God worshipped by his brother Moses. And given the imminent death of his own firstborn son, and the firstborn throughout Egypt, he would need strength to survive his own broken heart. How did God provide the strength Pharaoh needed for the softening of his heart? By forcing him to experience the grief of his own son's death, and later, to witness his soldiers' agony as they drowned.

After the death of his son, Pharaoh's broken heart opened him to God. This is what ultimately impelled him to liberate the Hebrew slaves. The hardening of his heart—by God or as an act of free will by Pharaoh—was necessary before he could change. Sometimes, when we act in ways that can harm others or ourselves, we need to be hammered at—reminded of the honorable path and strengthened through suffering—before we can freely choose to act in holy ways.

Brother from Another Mother—
Exodus 5:1–2

Afterward Moses and Aaron went to Pharaoh and said,
"Thus says the LORD, the God of Israel, 'Let my people go,
so that they may celebrate a festival to me in the wilderness.'"
But Pharaoh said, "Who is the LORD,
that I should heed him and let Israel go?
I do not know the LORD, and I will not let Israel go."

Each Easter since 1973, the ABC television network has shown Cecil
B. DeMille's 1956 epic film *The Ten Commandments* starring Charlton
Heston as Moses and Yul Brynner as Pharaoh. The most accurate aspect
of the film is that it was filmed in Egypt and the Sinai Peninsula, where
the Exodus took place. It has very few Jewish and Egyptian actors playing
the Jews and Egyptians, but the film is misleading in a more fundamental
way. It portrays an essentially non-familial, formal relationship between
Moses and Rameses, while according to the Torah Moses and Pharaoh
were raised together as stepbrothers.

Jewish tradition holds that these brothers had an intimate relationship throughout the first forty years of their lives. In contrast to
DeMille, their relationship is portrayed as close in the animated film
Moses, Prince of Egypt[42] because Disney hired a team of prominent Jewish
scholars and rabbis as consultants to the writers. You will see a beautiful portrayal of the loving relationship between the young Moses and
Rameses II. Using classical Jewish Midrash, the film has us imagine that
the two of them loved each other as they were being raised together.

So according to tradition, the meeting between Moses and Pharaoh
in Exodus 5 is an emotional reunion of two men who had not seen
each other in four decades. Let's review the story. Moses is born under
the decree from Rameses I to kill all the newborn Hebrew boys. Moses's

mother, Jochebed, places him in a basket and puts it in the reeds by the bank of the Nile River. His older sister, Miriam, keeps an eye on what happens. Pharaoh's daughter, Batya, sees the baby, recognizes that he is a Hebrew, and adopts him as her son.

The text of the book of Exodus is sparse on details, so commentators depend on Midrash and deductive reasoning to get the full story. Imagine what incredible courage it took for the princess to go against her own father's decree and adopt a Hebrew child. This is comparable to the daughter of Alabama's governor in 1850 adopting the baby of an African American slave. To make this plausible, we have to imagine Batya as a strong and influential young woman (living up to her name, which means daughter of God). Rabbi Maurice Harris points out the incredible irony: "Her name proclaims that the daughter of Pharaoh has been 'adopted' by the Hebrews' God as God's own daughter. In adopting the abandoned Hebrew baby she herself becomes adopted by Pharaoh's rival for true ultimate power in the world, God."[43]

In the Torah, the rescue of baby Moses results in three special relationships that are implied but not explicitly developed. Batya employs Moses's own mother to nurse the child (Exod. 2:9). We can imagine a close relationship between Jochebed, the biological mother, and Batya, the adoptive mother—what today we would call an open adoption. Further, we can deduce a close bond between Miriam, the big sister of Moses, and Batya, the big sister of Rameses II—destined to be Pharaoh someday. Finally, the intimate relationship between these two boys cannot be overstated. They are raised together, both as princes of Egypt. (To be precise, since Moses is adopted by Rameses's sister, this makes Rameses Moses's uncle, but they are raised as if they were brothers.)

As we read the story of Moses and Rameses, we are reminded of all the brother stories in Genesis, most of which did not go so well: Cain kills Abel; Ham is cursed to serve Shem and Japheth; Isaac is mocked by Ishmael; Jacob deceives his brother Esau; Joseph's brothers attempt to murder him.

Where is God in all this internecine strife? Providing the siblings with free will. God quietly asks Cain, "Where is Abel, your brother?" But Cain answers, "Am I my brother's keeper?" (With Hebrew syntax it reads, "The guardian of my brother am I?" It can be read as a question or a statement.) Cain's words echo throughout Genesis and Exodus, especially in the sibling rivalry stories. It is also a question for the entire nation of Egypt concerning its enslaved Hebrew population. And it's a question between Pharaoh and Moses. They are from different ethnic backgrounds, different continents (Asia and Africa), and different religious traditions.

When Moses fled from Egypt, did Rameses II hear the voice of God saying, "Where is your brother?" Did he grow bitter and begin to think, "Am I my brother's keeper?" We ought to imagine this reunion forty years later not as a meeting between the head of state and the leader of a slave rebellion but as a tense yet intimate encounter between two brothers who once loved each other, who have not seen each other in decades, and who have grown apart in so many ways. Moses is saying, in effect, that he is his brother's keeper, concerning not just the slaves, but also his brother, Pharaoh. Rameses refuses to recognize the God of Moses who asks, "Where is your brother?" Some brothers in Genesis eventually reconcile. We are left to wonder whether Moses and Rameses II ever will.

Redemption for Egypt—Exodus 7:5

The Egyptians shall know that I am the LORD.

One of the most profound elements of the civil rights movement of the 1950s and 1960s is the emphasis by black religious leaders that redemption was not just for the victim, but for the victimizer as well. The Reverend Martin Luther King and other African American pastors taught that the movement was not only for the redemption of Black Americans, but that their liberation would lead to the liberation of White Americans from their racism. Rooted firmly in the story of Exodus, Rev. King preached:

> Let us remember that as we struggle against Egypt, we must have love, compassion and understanding goodwill for those against whom we struggle, helping them to realize that as we seek to defeat the evils of Egypt we are not seeking to defeat them but to help them, as well as ourselves.[44]

Based on the story of the Hebrews and Pharaoh, King understood the principle that the liberation of the oppressed by the oppressor is dependent on the oppressor being liberated from his oppressiveness—not defeated but liberated. Today, the Dalai Lama has a similar view of the liberation of Tibet from the Chinese. He has taught that the Tibetan people cannot be truly free from being oppressed until the Chinese government is free from its own oppressiveness. He has told this story on several occasions:

> A senior monk I know spent 17–18 years in Chinese prison after 1959. In the 1980s he was released and was able to join me in India. Once, when we were chatting about his experiences

he told me that there had been dangerous moments during his imprisonment. I thought he meant threats to his life, but he said, "No, there were times when there was a danger of my losing compassion for my Chinese captors."[45]

The same principle of compassion is taught in both the Elder and Younger Testaments. In a Midrash it is taught, "Who is a leader? Any person who can turns an enemy into one's friend."[46] Rabbi Jesus taught this principle when he said, "You have heard it was said, 'You shall love your neighbor and hate your enemy.' But I say to you, 'Love your enemies and pray for those who persecute you'" (Matt. 5:43–44).

Concern for the liberation of the oppressor is an important Jewish principle on an individual level, and it also has been important for the Jewish people as they have dealt with one oppressive empire after another. We can easily find these principles in classical Jewish teachings on the Exodus. The primary goal of the Exodus is the liberation of Hebrew slaves. The intent of Moses, Aaron, and Miriam is to liberate the Jews; this is obvious. But their underlying aim is to also redeem Egypt, the nation where they had been born, raised, acculturated, and educated. Thus, the second principle is just as important: to free the Egyptians from being slaveholders. It is inspiring to see how often God makes it clear to Moses that the Egyptians too must be set free. Moses, the sages, the rabbis, and Rev. King understood that there was no liberation for the Jews from slavery until Pharaoh and all of Egypt were redeemed from an economic system that was based on the subjugation of one people by another.

There are many passages in the Tanakh that imply or clearly state that one of the goals of the Exodus was to redeem Egypt and its citizens:

Exodus 14:18: And the Egyptians shall know that I am the LORD, when I have gained glory for myself over Pharaoh, his chariots, and his chariot drivers.

Isaiah 19:23–25: On that day there will be a highway from Egypt to Assyria, and the Assyrian will come into Egypt, and the Egyptian into Assyria, and the Egyptians will worship with the Assyrians. On that day Israel will be the third with Egypt and Assyria, a blessing in the midst of the earth, whom the Lord of hosts has blessed, saying, "Blessed be Egypt my people, and Assyria the work of my hands, and Israel my heritage."

Ezekiel 29:6: Then all the inhabitants of Egypt shall know that I am the Lord because you were a staff of reed to the house of Israel.[47]

Jews and Christians often overlook the universal nature of the prophecy in Isaiah 19, especially the last verse: "Blessed be Egypt my people, and Assyria the work of my hands, and Israel my heritage." We know that Israel is called God's heritage. But most commentators don't dwell on God calling Egypt "my people," or Assyria being called "the work of my hands." These empires were often the oppressors of the Jewish people, but the prophet sees a time when Egypt, Assyria, and Israel will all be blessed with a highway running between them. May we see that highway built in our lifetime.

Pharaoh's National Repentance Movement—Exodus 9:27–28

Then Pharaoh summoned Moses and Aaron, and said to them,
"This time I have sinned; the LORD is in the right, and I and my people are in
the wrong. Pray to the LORD! Enough of God's thunder and hail! I will let you
go..."

When Pharaoh finally sees the error of his ways, it feels like a miracle. But no sooner has he let the Israelites go than he changes his mind. The Torah says, "When Pharaoh saw that the rain and the hail and the thunder had ceased, he sinned once more and hardened his heart . . . and he would not let the Israelites go" (Exod. 9:34, 35). Many of us, like Pharaoh, have learned the hard way that repentance is not a straight path from sin to atonement. More often it's two steps forward and one step back.

Rameses II was raised to believe he was the incarnation of the sun god Ra, with power and wealth beyond anything we can imagine. When his ego is challenged by his stepbrother Moses, he must be thinking: who is this Moses that I once foolishly called my brother? A Hebrew from an enslaved people! Not even a real, true-blooded Egyptian! For Rameses's heart to open again, something tragic will have to happen.

It is only after the tenth plague, when he feels the heartbreak of his own firstborn son's death, that Rameses yields to the God of Israel and liberates the Hebrews. Yet within a week of their emancipation, he regrets his decision and sends his top charioteers after them. Two steps forward, one step back. He is clearly in the throes of inner turmoil. As we know, the sea parts for Moses, the children of Israel cross in safety, and the Egyptian soldiers drown.

One Midrash suggests that Pharaoh was actually the lone survivor of the charioteers. The famous "Song at the Sea," chanted with Moses leading the men and Miriam leading the women, includes the words "Who is like you, O LORD, among the gods? Who is like you, majestic in holiness?" (Exod. 15:11). The Midrash proposes that Moses chanted, "Who is like you, O LORD, among the gods," but it is Rameses who responds with the second part of the verse, "Who is like you, majestic in holiness?" This is a transformative moment for Pharaoh as he repents for his arrogance right there. In his emotional torment, still mourning the deaths of his son and soldiers, he calls out to God, "Who is like you, majestic in holiness?" He finally recognizes the God of his brother, the God of Israel, as the true Deity. In this Midrash, there is liberation for the oppressed and the oppressor.

If we accept the possibility of Pharaoh's survival, the question arises: if he did live, why does the Torah never mention him again? A second fascinating Midrash suggests that after the incident at the Red Sea, Pharaoh flees Egypt to later become king of Nineveh, the Assyrian city God would later be sending Jonah to. Dr. Raphael Zarum teaches: "When the prophet Jonah showed up, Pharaoh immediately led a national repentance movement. . . . Thus Pharaoh becomes the paradigm of change that we read about and learn from every *Yom Kippur*."[48]

Unlike Amalek, a character whom the rabbis deem as the archetype of unredeemable evil, Pharaoh is considered the model of a bad person who is capable of change. In his moments of passion and emotional wavering throughout the Exodus story, he reveals an inner torment that is recognizably human. The Midrashim of his atonement tell a parallel tale of metamorphoses from tyrant to liberator, and ultimately to leading a national redemption movement. These interpretations, as farfetched as they may seem, reflect back to us the remarkable possibilities of rising above our own limitations.

The Ten Plagues—Exodus 11:1

The LORD said to Moses,
"I will bring one more plague upon Pharaoh and upon Egypt;
afterwards he will let you go."

Midway through every Passover seder, the ten plagues are plaintively chanted. The leader of the ceremony calls out the name of each of the ten plagues that ravaged Egypt, and the participants echo the name of each plague as they spill a drop of wine onto their empty plates. Wine at the Passover seder generally brings joy, but spilling the drops reminds us to diminish our joy in acknowledgment of the suffering of the Egyptians.

Blood, Frogs, Lice, Flies, Pestilence, Boils, Hail,
Locusts, Darkness, Death of the firstborn.

First-century Jewish philosopher Philo of Alexandria was renowned for his allegorical interpretations of the Tanakh. Of the first plague, the Nile River turning to blood, he said: "Praiseworthy speech is likened to a river; but speech which is deserving of blame is the very river of Egypt itself, intractable, unwilling to learn, as one may say in a word, lifeless speech; for which reason it is also changed into blood, as not being able to afford sustenance."[49]

In the Tanakh, we often see curses coupled with their corrections—their aim is to rectify and heal. In Egypt, the Nile was believed to be a god since its waters gave sustenance to the land, so the plague of blood is seen as a correction for the misplaced worship, and a redirection of attention to God. According to Philo, "The vivifying power of the river was changed to a destructive power . . . until the Egyptians entreated Moses, and Moses entreated God."[50] Each successive plague is coupled with a rectification.

In the second century, the early Christian theologian Origen also examined the plagues allegorically. Dr. Scott Langston summarizes Origen's interpretations: "The various plagues demonstrate the conquering of certain undesirable worldly elements."[51] Water turning to blood represents secular philosophy. Frogs correspond to worldly songs and poetry. Lice represent the "deceptive art of dialectic." Flies stand for worldly pleasure. Pestilence symbolizes making animals into idols. Boils point to "the judgment on malice, pride, and anger." Hail stands for vice. Locusts represent "the inability of rational humans to rule themselves . . . or submit to God as king." Darkness stands for intellectual blindness. Finally, the death of the firstborn symbolizes "false religions." Langston goes on to explain:

> Origen not only understood the plagues within the context of the larger world . . . he also applied them to the individual (reflecting the moral meaning). These events illustrate how a person, living ignorant of the truth in the world (Egypt), is freed. The soul's initial impulses to sin must be destroyed by God's Law, and once this is accomplished, the individual can join the Israelite people in their exodus from Egypt. Origen has essentially refashioned the plague narrative from a national experience to a personal one that describes how an individual becomes a member of God's people.[52]

Many commentators interpret the plagues psychologically as the stages in the struggle to get out of "personal Egypts"—emotional constrictions. In this way the plagues are not merely divine punishments but necessary stages leading to personal liberation. Every person goes through ten stages/plagues in the struggle to be free from an oppressive condition or relationship. Dr. Robert Rosenthal teaches: "The plagues are the spasms of suffering—the labor pains, if you will—that the ego will endure and try to overcome before it finally surrenders."[53]

Renowned Rabbi Menachem Schneerson uses the same allegorical method as Philo and Origen, almost two thousand years later:

The first plague to break the Egyptian exile was that of blood.
. . . Water is a substance that is cold and moist. Coldness
generally symbolizes the opposite of holiness. Holiness stands
for vitality. . . . These waters of the Nile (i.e. the coldness
toward holiness) constitute the idolatry of Egypt. . . . The
first plague converted those waters into blood. Blood indicates
vitality as it is said "for the blood is the life force."[54]

Rabbi Schneerson urges people to turn their own water into blood—
to transform personal coldness (water) into passion for holiness (blood).
He describes the psychological meaning of the second plague of frogs:

In carrying out their mission they [the frogs] demonstrated
the sublime or holy coldness toward physical and material
things. . . . in order to leave, and rid ourselves of the impure
'egypt' we must introduce warmth and vitality into everything
relating to holiness; for coldness is the beginning of all
sorts of evil. . . . In order to rid oneself of 'egypt' one must
remember that first comes 'blood'—the ardent involvement
with holiness. . . .[55]

The twentieth-century Jungian psychologist Dr. Edward Edinger
interpreted the plagues as part of a process known as *individuation*—the
full integration of the psyche wherein the collective unconscious shared
by all humanity is brought into consciousness. He offers the symbolic
psychological meaning for each plague:

Blood: "the welling up of violent affects. In one of the
last plagues of the Apocalypse the sea is turned to blood
(Revelation 16:3)."

Frogs: "the primordial 'swamp level' of the psyche—primitive,
slimy, cold-blooded contents which invade consciousness."

Lice and Flies: "the activated unconscious as provoking an irritable, restless state of agitation."

Pestilence: "The death of a large animal . . . in a dream is a matter of grave concern. It means that one's major instinctual foundation has been lost and it may harbinger physical illness or even death."

Boils: "festering unconscious complexes requiring drainage (abreaction)."

Hail: "the frozen state of the feeling life in which warm and living impulses are congealed by the power motive. In Dante's imagery, Lucifer resides in the depths of hell embedded in ice."

Locusts: "Invasion by insects is an image of being overrun by a multiplicity of elementary units. It indicates a fragmentation of the psyche on an elemental level."

Darkness: "Now the light of consciousness is completely eclipsed."

Death of the Firstborn: "The events of Passover night present an awesome image of an encounter with the activated Self . . . Passover symbolism repeats itself in a new context with the death of Christ. He takes upon himself the fate of the Egyptian firstborn and of the Paschal Lamb."[56]

The late Rabbi Aryeh Hirschfield and I used to speak about the death of the firstborn sons as the death of "firstborn, self-limiting consciousness within each person." By about five years old, people have a sense of their limitations, and it's this self-limitation that must "die" for the individual to be liberated and achieve his or her God-given potential.

At the Passover seder, the chanting of the tenth plague inevitably evokes shock, sadness, and empathy for the Egyptian families who suffered the loss of their sons. Most people can appreciate allegorical interpretations of the plagues, but the idea that God punished innocent firstborn sons of Egypt is still difficult to grasp. We might justify this plague as a reciprocal response to the previous Pharaoh's edict to kill newborn Hebrew boys, or perhaps see it as appropriate punishment for hundreds of years of slavery.

Or, maybe we can conclude it is in the Torah for the same reason as the story of Abraham nearly killing his son Isaac—for us to push against and argue with God that it's simply unjust. Jews see arguing with God as making us better people, truer servants of the Holy. When we rail against horrific treatment by God, or any character, in the Torah or in life, we draw closer to our own humanity, our innate godliness. Our vehement arguments and myriad interpretations are part of the fabric of the Jewish spiritual path.

Wholeheartedly examining the symbolism of the plagues in the Exodus story can be a gateway of discovery to our own inner freedom.

Four Opinions at the Shoreline—
Exodus 14:9

The Egyptians pursued them, all Pharaoh's horses and chariots,
his chariot drivers and his army; they overtook them camped by the sea.

There's a Jewish saying: "Two Jews, four opinions." From the start, Jews have been arguing with each other and with God about how the Scriptures are to be applied to daily life. In the Tanakh, Abraham is the first to argue with God. Moses stands up to God; Hannah, Elijah, and Hezekiah plead with God; and Job brazenly challenges God. In the Talmud and rabbinic tradition, debate has been elevated to the level of a sacred art. The name Israel even means God-wrestler. So, when the children of Israel reach the shore of the Red Sea, what do they do? They argue about what comes next, and the Midrash unpacks what happens in detail.

Just seven days after he let the Hebrews go free, Pharaoh had second thoughts. The Torah tells us he went after the people with six hundred premier chariots, plus the rest of the Egyptian army's chariots. The Hebrew people, stuck at the shoreline of the Red Sea and hearing the clamor of the chariots approaching, start arguing. One group believes that prayer is needed: "In great fear the Israelites cried out to the LORD" (Exod. 14:10). A second group wants to be holy martyrs and commit suicide: "You have taken us away to die in the wilderness" (Exod. 14:11). A third group wishes to return to Egypt where at least there was food and shelter: "Let us alone and let us serve the Egyptians" (Exod. 14:12). A fourth group suggests fighting the Egyptian army, but Moses tells them, "The LORD will fight for you, and you have only to keep still" (Exod. 14:14). Even Moses isn't certain how to take action, so he sides with the group advocating prayer. When he prays, though, God says, "Why do you cry out to me?" (Exod. 14:15). God disagreed with the opinions of all four groups.

One of the most crucial words in the Torah appears in the next verse. The word is *v'yisa-oo*, meaning "go forward" or "journey on." God tells the people not to return to Egypt, not to fight, not to martyr themselves, and not even to pray. There may be an appropriate time for each of these choices, but now is the time to take a leap of faith and go forward. God says this knowing that the people cannot swim across the Red Sea.

The Talmud tells us that when God commands the people to "go forward," no one wants to be the first to step into the sea (Sotah 37a).[57] Naturally, they fear drowning. At that moment, a little-known Jewish hero named Nachshon ben Aminadav, Aaron's brother-in-law, steps out in front of the people and walks into the sea. First, he wades in up to his knees, then up to his chest, and then all the way up to his neck. Nothing happens. Nachshon continues, walking so far that the water covers his lips, and still nothing happens. But when his nose is covered so there was no way to breathe, then and only then does the sea begin to part. The Midrash tells us that it is in the merit of Nachshon's tremendous act of faith that both King David and the Messiah would descend from his lineage.

The image of Nachshon's unrelenting courage and belief in God stands out in Jewish tradition as a powerful metaphor. When we are faced with what seems like an impossible obstacle, we can listen to God's call, "Journey on. Go forward!" and summon a little bit of Nachshon's faith. Only then will the sea part for us.

Grief and Joy at the Seashore— Exodus 14:30

Thus the LORD saved Israel that day from the Egyptians;
and Israel saw the Egyptians dead on the seashore.

The Torah says that "Israel saw the Egyptians dead on the seashore." Can you imagine standing on a shore where dead body after dead body of your enemy is washing up on the sand? What would you feel? What would any person feel? Proverbs 11:10 reports the natural inclination of people to be jubilant: "When it goes well with the righteous, the city rejoices; and when the wicked perish, there is jubilation." But, on the other hand, in Proverbs 24:17 it is taught, "Do not rejoice when your enemies fall, and do not let your heart be glad when they stumble." How difficult the latter instruction is to follow. Success naturally calls forth celebration, yet both Jewish and Christian traditions emphasize the need to have compassion even for those who have harmed us.

As mentioned earlier (page 70), each year at seders around the world, while participants rejoice in reimagining the story of liberation, when reciting the plagues that devastated the Egyptians participants take time to remember the suffering of those who oppressed them. When the story of Pharaoh's charioteers drowning in the sea is retold, we temper any inclination to rejoice.

There is a popular anecdote from the Talmud. When Pharaoh's army drowned in the Red Sea, the angels in heaven were singing along with Moses, Miriam, and the children of Israel and saw that God was weeping. They asked, "Holy One, why are you crying when your children, the Hebrews, have just crossed the Sea?" The Holy One replied, "Why are you singing when the works of my hands, the Egyptians, have just drowned?"[58]

Dr. Raphael Zarum offers a powerful metaphor:

> We have to live with this dichotomy. If we are not happy
> that evil has been punished, then we do not care enough,
> but if we are not sad at the loss of life, then our humanity is
> weakened. . . . Maybe the dramatic image of the sea splitting
> is the actual metaphor for this dichotomy. The two shores
> of the sea represent the two sides of the story. And we must
> pass through the middle, preserving and valuing life, yet not
> drowning in war and hate. The middle path between justice
> and mercy is a difficult one to tread and at any moment we can
> be washed away.[59]

To Christian interpreters of Scripture, the passage across the Red
Sea is seen as a prefiguration of the ritual of baptism, and the drowning
of Pharaoh's soldiers represents the death of sin. To the rabbis, and
especially the Jewish mystics, Pharaoh represents an aspect of human
character where repentance and change is possible. Rabbi Lawrence
Kushner puts it beautifully: "What drowns in the Red Sea is not Pharaoh
and his armies, but an aspect of the ego. It is reabsorbed into the
personality, but forever gone as a dynamic force."[60]

Today, the media bombard us with images of carnage through war
and natural disasters, and we tend to be hardened to death and human
suffering, not unlike Pharaoh. Sometimes it is the dynamic force of our
compassion that gets drowned. We need to be constantly reminded that
every person is a child of God, created in the image of God—to take
these ancient Bible stories to heart, to let them challenge us, and soften
our hardened hearts so that the dynamic force of our inner pharaohs can
be transformed and replaced by the dynamic force of compassion.

The Top Ten—Exodus 20:1–17

1. *I am the LORD your God*
2. *You shall not make for yourself an idol*
3. *You shall not make wrongful use*
   of the name of the LORD
4. *Remember the Sabbath day*
5. *Honor your father and your mother*
6. *You shall not murder*
7. *You shall not commit adultery*
8. *You shall not steal*
9. *You shall not bear false witness*
10. *You shall not covet*

Forty-nine days after they were freed from captivity the Hebrews were camped at the foot of Mount Sinai preparing to receive the Revelation from God. On the fiftieth night after the first day of Passover ends, Jews commemorate this event with the Festival of *Shavuot* (called Pentecost in Greek or the Festival of Weeks). They say special prayers, read the book of Ruth, and attend synagogue to hear the chanting of the Ten Commandments from a Torah scroll.

Jews, Orthodox Christians, Catholics, and Protestants each follow a slightly different list of the Ten Commandments. In the Pentateuch, there are actually 613 commandments: 248 positive "Thou shalts," and 365 negative "Thou shalt nots." The Ten Commandments, as important as they are, are simply a summary of them all. In Matthew 22:37, Jesus joins a Jewish discussion that was common during the first century about which *mitzvot* are the most important. Rabbi Akiva says the greatest is, "You shall love your neighbor as yourself" (Lev. 19:18). Jesus suggests there are two: "You shall love the LORD your God with all your heart, and with all your soul, and with all your might" (Deut. 6:5) and "You shall love your neighbor as yourself."[61]

The first four of the Ten Commandments represent "love the Lord"—the relationship between a person and God. The last five commandments represent "love your neighbor"—the relationship between a person and others. The fifth commandment, "Honor your father and mother," bridges the divide between people's relationships with God and with each other.

More narrowly, Jewish tradition suggests looking at the Ten Commandments as broad categories in which all the other 603 commandments fit. For example, all the commandments to observe holidays (Passover, New Year, Day of Atonement, Succoth, Shavuot, etc.) would fall under the *mitzvah* to "remember the Sabbath day," since all holidays are like Sabbaths. The prohibitions against gossip and slander in Leviticus would fall under "You shall not murder" and "You shall not steal," since the misuse of speech metaphorically murders or steals a person's reputation.

There are many commentaries about what the people actually heard during the theophany at Sinai. A classic second-century commentary called the *Mekhilta* follows a very literal interpretation of the word "all" in the verse "God spoke *all* these words" (Exod. 20:1), and suggests that they heard all Ten Commandments simultaneously in a miraculous single utterance. The great eleventh-century commentator Rashi says that after the single utterance God spoke the first two commandments directly to the people. Everyone became terrified and asked Moses to say the remaining eight: "[The people] were afraid and trembled and stood at a distance, and said to Moses, 'You speak to us, and we will listen; but do not let God speak to us, or we will die'" (Exod. 20:18–19).

A covenant is a contract between two parties. The term *testament*, used to describe both the Jewish and Christian Scriptures, comes from the Latin for "covenant." The Mosaic covenant was ratified by the Hebrews on behalf of all future generations of the Jewish people with a simple and beautiful statement: "Then he [Moses] took the book of the covenant, and read it in the hearing of the people; and they said, 'All that the LORD has spoken we will do, and we will be obedient'" (Exod. 24:7). The word *nishma* translated here as "we will be obedient" literally means "we will hear," and by implication "we will understand." This phrase is interpreted to mean, "We'll perform the commandments first and after doing them we'll be able to understand them." Jewish tradition teaches that it took incredible faith for the newly emancipated slave population to say they would "do" the commandments before they really understood them.

On Shavuot, many Jewish communities, especially Sephardic ones, reenact a wedding ceremony when the Ten Commandments are chanted aloud in synagogue. The bride and groom are the Jewish people and the Holy One, respectively. Congregants respond to each commandment as if it were a marriage vow saying the exact words from the Torah, *na-aseh v'nishmah*—we will do and hear. A *ketubah* (marriage contract) is read that clearly enumerates the obligations of God to the Jewish people. As in any good marriage, it takes faith to agree to each other's vows. Following is an abridged version of a popular *ketubah* read on Shavuot. It was written by sixteenth-century mystic poet Israel Najara in the city of Safed:

> The Invisible One came forth from Sinai . . . in the year 2448 since the creation. The Bridegroom, Ruler of rulers said unto the pious, lovely and virtuous bride, the people of Israel, who won His favor who is beautiful as the moon, radiant as the sun, awesome as bannered hosts: "Be thou My mate according to the law of Moses and Israel, and I will honor, support, and maintain thee and be thy shelter and refuge in everlasting mercy."
>
> This bride, Israel, consented and became His spouse. Thus an eternal covenant, binding them forever, was established between them. The Bridegroom then agreed to add to the above all future expositions of Scripture. The dowry that this bride brought from the house of her father consists of an understanding heart that understands, ears that hearken, and eyes that see. All these conditions are valid and established forever and ever.

I invoke heaven and earth as reliable witnesses. May the Bridegroom rejoice with the bride whom He has taken as His lot and may the bride rejoice with the Husband of her youth while uttering words of praise.[62]

God Spoke?—Exodus 20:1–2

Then God spoke all these words:
I am the LORD your God, who brought you out of the land of Egypt,
out of the house of slavery.

Rabbi Meshulam Zusha of Hanipol is an eighteenth-century ecstatic mystic known as Zusha. It is said that once, as a student, while his fellow students were having a serious debate about the meaning of a verse in the Torah, Zusha fell into an ecstatic state, rocking back and forth, mumbling inaudible sounds. A friend turned to him and asked, "Are you OK?" Zusha answered, "Yes, I'm OK. More than OK. Look what it says in the Torah. God *spoke* to Moses . . . God *spoke* to . . . *God Spoke.* Isn't that amazing? . . . *God Spoke!*" While the others were exploring the intricacies of the whole text, Zusha was awestruck at just the first two words. He couldn't get over the idea that the Holy One actually spoke.

But, how does God speak? There are numerous places in the Pentateuch where we read, "And the LORD *spoke* to Moses saying," but does God speak words as humans do, out loud? Unlikely. To say "God speaks" is our anthropomorphic description of something that transcends physical language. Divine transmission, filtered through the human mind, may be metaphorically described as speech, but it transcends actual vocalization, emanating from the source of creation itself.

The rabbis called the Ten Commandments *Aseret HaDibrot*, literally meaning The Ten Words. The word for "speech" also means "thing," so The Ten Words could be translated as The Ten Things. Why didn't they use the Hebrew word *mitzvot* meaning "commandments"? Our biblical ancestors clearly sensed an intrinsic link between words and things. When the Holy One speaks in the ongoing act of creation, the world comes into existence and becomes matter.

In the Torah, when God creates the world by divine decree, it is framed as speech. In Genesis, there are ten instances when the Creator says, "Let there be" and there was. God says, "Let there be light," and there was light. As simple as that! The Holy One speaks, and the world comes into existence and becomes matter. When the Holy One spoke the Ten Commandments at Sinai, each commandment became a unique spiritual substance made manifest in the physical world. The psalmist tells us: "By the word of the LORD the heavens were made, and all their host by the breath of his mouth" (Ps. 33:6). This idea would later become the foundation for John telling us: "In the beginning was the Word, and the Word was with God, and the Word was God" (John 1:1).

The question then is the same one God asks us today: Does God speaking have real substance in your life, or, is it merely a quaint, anachronistic metaphor? Think of Zusha in ecstasy over the words "God spoke" and reach the place inside yourself where you realize the Creator speaks to you in every moment, in a constant renewal of creation.

They Saw Sounds—Exodus 20:18

When all the people witnessed the thunder and lightning,
the sound of the trumpet, and the mountain smoking,
they were afraid and trembled and stood at a distance.

When the children of Israel came to Mount Sinai just before the Ten Commandments were spoken, the Torah reports: "On the morning of the third day there was thunder and lightning, as well as a thick cloud on the mountain, and a blast of a trumpet so loud that all the people who were in the camp trembled" (Exod. 19:16).

The Hebrew words translated as "thunder" and "sound" also mean "voice." The people were *hearing* voices. A more literal translation is "On the morning of the third day there was a *voice* and lightning, as well as a thick cloud on the mountain, and a *voice* of a trumpet so loud that all the people who were in the camp trembled."

In Exodus 20:18, which occurs after the Ten Commandments were given, it implies that the children of Israel were in a transcendent state. As before, the word for "thunder" means "voices," so a more accurate translation is "all the people *saw* voices."

Seeing sounds is a neurological phenomenon called synesthesia—where the stimulation of one sensory organ is experienced as another sense. It is somewhat common for artists and musicians where the stimulation of one sensory organ is experienced as another sense. They might describe hearing colors, seeing sounds, or tasting touch.

It seems that after experiencing the astounding communal revelation of the Ten Commandments, the Hebrews experienced mass synesthesia—their senses transposing as in music when changing from one key to another. No wonder the Torah tells us "they were afraid and trembled, and stood at a distance." Wouldn't we all?

A Calf of Gold—Exodus 32:1

When the people saw that Moses delayed to come down from the mountain,
the people gathered around Aaron, and said to him,
"Come, make gods for us, who shall go before us."

The Hebrews trembled in awe as the voice of YHVH emerged from a sound-and-light show with smoke, fire, thunder, and lightning. It is the first time in recorded history that an entire population experienced a theophany together. The Ten Commandments—the code of living that delineates human relationships to God and to each other—had just been revealed to them at Mount Sinai.

After the theophany, the rabbis tell us, the people miscalculated Moses's return date by a mere day. In that short time, though, a small but influential group who thought they no longer had a leader succumbed to panic. They asked, "Who shall go before us; as for this Moses, the man who brought us up out of the land of Egypt, we do not know what has become of him" (Exod. 32:1). The tradition tells us Aaron consented to build an idol only because he knew Moses would return, and he could use the time it would take to melt the gold and make the calf as a delaying tactic. When Aaron saw the people beginning to worship the idol, though, he tried to dissuade them by saying, "Tomorrow shall be a festival to the LORD" (Ex. 32:5).

But why did the Hebrews choose a calf for the idol? The bull was a prevalent religious symbol throughout North Africa and the Middle East. It was a common icon of worship in Egypt where the bull was believed to be a god, so the group could have been reverting to the "old time religion" from their captivity. The first letter of the Egyptian pictographic alphabet was a depiction of a bull. (This was adopted by Hebrews as their first letter *aleph*, later called *alpha* in Greek. Our modern letter A, in fact, derives from that original pictograph of a bull.)

This incident occurred at the end of what astrologers call Taurus—the astrological sign represented by the bull. The liberation of the Hebrew slaves occurred during Aries, represented by the ram.* As Judaism developed, the image of the ram took prominence. The ram was prevalent in its stories (the binding of Isaac), in its economy (many Hebrews were shepherds), and in religious symbols (the ram's horn, the Torah scroll made of sheep skin, etc.). The ram symbol was embedded in daily and religious life, but was not an actual representation of god, as was the image of the bull in Egypt. The group of people who demanded that Aaron make a golden calf wanted a god with a visible image. They were not ready to embrace the abstract notion of an invisible, omniscient, single deity who spoke to them from a mountain, demanding strict adherence to a moral code of behavior.

The story of Aaron and the golden calf is a cautionary tale that still rings true today. We all want the comfort of what we know, of doing things the old-fashioned way. But the story of Exodus moves forward—God commands the Hebrews to journey on and not to return to the familiar gods of Egypt. This story teaches us that staying in our comfort zones will not move us into deeper alignment with ourselves or with God. Ask yourself: What are the "familiar gods of Egypt"—the comfortable behaviors—that I cling to? What kind of "golden calf" do I fashion when I fear going into new territory in my life?

---

* In ancient times astrology was an attempt to make sense of the movement of the stars and planets, and to discern their possible influences in the natural world, in events such as eclipses. Jewish and Christian theologians like St. Augustine, St. Thomas Aquinas, and Rabbi Akiva embraced the aspects of astrology that were rooted in natural science (while dismissing its use as a tool for divination of future events or personality analysis). There is clear evidence in the Talmud, however, that at least some of the early rabbis believed that each of the twelve months, with its associated astrological sign, could portend good or bad fortune. Images of the zodiac appear in early Jewish and Christian art. (Mosaic tiles depicting the zodiac have been preserved throughout the Middle East on synagogue floors, reflecting its use as a central decorative motif in the Talmudic period, about 200 BCE to 500 CE.)

Spies, Heroes, and Grasshoppers—
Numbers 13:1–2

> *The LORD said to Moses, "Send men to spy out the land of Canaan,*
> *which I am giving to the Israelites;*
> *from each of their ancestral tribes you shall send a man,*
> *every one a leader among them."*

God knew in the first days of the Exodus that the Hebrews who had been enslaved for so long were weary and broken in spirit. Exodus 13:17 reports, "When Pharaoh let the people go, God did not lead them by way of the land of the Philistines, although that was nearer; for God thought, 'If the people face war, they may change their minds and return to Egypt.'" After the miracle of crossing the Red Sea followed by the revelation of the Ten Commandments, the people stayed in the vicinity of Mount Sinai for a year to absorb and internalize the recent miraculous occurrences. In the second year after leaving Egypt, God hoped their spirits would be restored enough to go forward and enter Canaan.

God instructed Moses to send leaders of each of the twelve tribes to check out the land and report back about its condition and its inhabitants. Although the Hebrews had come from Canaan (and Mesopotamia), hundreds of years of enslavement in a foreign land had severed their ties to the land. The scouts were to assess potential military resistance from the non-Hebrews living there, as well as the quality of the land—the forests and its agricultural produce.

The expression "wide-eyed" is an apt description for the experience of the scouts. To them, everything in Canaan, including the people, looked huge and monstrous. The Torah reports that a single cluster of grapes was so big it had to be carried on a pole between two men. This so impressed the scouts that, "that place was called the Wadi Eshcol, because of the cluster that the Israelites cut down from there" (Num. 13:24). They brought back samples of the oversized produce to Moses and the Hebrews, and gave what most commentators call an "evil" or "bad" report.

Interestingly, everything the scouts said about the land and its inhabitants was true, but they spun it in such a way that it aroused fear and doubt in the minds of the people, saying "the towns are fortified and very large" (Num. 13:28). They reported, "We saw the Nephilim [giants]; and to ourselves we seemed like grasshoppers, and so we seemed to them" (Num. 13:33). They may have been strong and capable, but their diminished self-image projected only weakness to the Nephilim.

Since the Hebrews had only been emancipated for a year, the last thing they wanted was to engage in a military battle to settle on the land. Scouts Joshua and Caleb tried to calm the people's fears—"Let us go up at once and occupy it, for we are well able to overcome it" (Num. 13:30)—but it was too late, the people were agitated and terrified.

A year earlier, while Moses was receiving the Ten Commandments on Mount Sinai, he took longer to return than expected. Losing faith in their leader, the people built a golden calf and reverted to the idol worship they were familiar with in Egypt. Moses quelled God's anger, "and the LORD changed his mind about the disaster that he planned to bring on his people" (Exod. 32:14).

Angered again after the spies' distorted report, God responds to Moses's plea for mercy: "I do forgive, just as you have asked; nevertheless . . . none of the people who have seen my glory and the signs that I did in Egypt and in the wilderness . . . shall see the land that I swore to give to their ancestors" (Num. 14:20–23). With the exception of Joshua and Caleb, the entire first generation of emancipated slaves would live out their lives in exile and die in the wilderness. Rather than entering the land in the second year of the Exodus, the people would journey from campsite to campsite over a period of forty years. God said, "According to the number of the days in which you spied out the land, forty days, for every day a year, you shall bear your iniquity, forty years, and you shall know my displeasure" (Num. 14:34).

Jewish tradition says the spies gave their bad report on the ninth day in the month of Av (called *Tisha B'Av* in Hebrew), and this date has had horrific reverberations throughout Jewish history. On this date, both the first and second temples in Jerusalem were destroyed; the First Crusade started in 1096; Jews were expelled from England (1290), France (1306), and Spain (1492); and the mass deportation of Jews from the Warsaw ghetto to concentration camps occurred in 1942. Tisha B'Av is the most mournful day in the Jewish calendar. However, the sages and rabbis also suggest that hope must arise out of so many catastrophes, saying Tisha B'Av is to be the birthday of the future Messiah.

When we examine the sin of the spies and the response of the people, it may not seem so grievous, but such a level of self-doubt and fear ultimately would have been self-destructive. God wanted this emerging nation to be brave and go forward. The Hebrews were subverting their own destiny. The negative report of the spies ignited an epidemic of fear among the people that blinded them to what God wanted from them and for them.

The metaphor, of course, is obvious and painfully relevant. For each of us, our deepest work is to remain in touch with what God wants from us. It takes enormous courage to quell our self-doubt and quiet the negative voices that get in the way of being true to ourselves. As spiritual seekers, we sometimes feel that we wander from campsite to campsite, always trying to enter the land. No matter what our religion, our spiritual practices and prayer offer a way to continually tune out those voices and turn toward the voice of God. When we are afraid to take the next step in our lives, we can find strength in the story of the spies. We can remember that God's image of us is never diminished, and it is our sacred task to see ourselves as God sees us, strong and whole.

In a Wilderness of Words and Things— Deuteronomy 2:7

Surely the LORD *your God has blessed you in all your undertakings;*
he knows your going through this great wilderness.
These forty years the LORD *your God has been with you; you have lacked*
nothing.

The Hebrews sensed an energetic connection between the wilderness, words, and material things. The biblical word *wilderness* is *midbar*, and the words for speech and thing both come from the same root (*devar*). To hear the Word of God, our biblical heroes went into the wilderness where they were able to get away from their preoccupation with the material things of day-to-day life. In the nineteenth century, Mary Baker Eddy described the wilderness experience of the children of Israel in both personal and transcendent terms as a journey between the worlds of our physical sensations and our souls. She wrote:

> As the children of Israel were guided triumphantly through the Red Sea—the dark ebbing and flowing tides of human fear—as they were led through the wilderness, walking wearily through the great desert of human hopes, and anticipating the promised joy, so shall the spiritual idea guide all right desires in their passage from sense to Soul, from a material sense of existence to the spiritual, up to the glory prepared for them who love God.[63]

The wilderness is a liminal zone between the natural and spiritual worlds, a place where one can more easily commune with the Creator. Transcendent moments in the Torah frequently occur in the wilderness:

the burning bush, the Ten Commandments, Moses's death, Isaiah's vision of a highway, and Jesus being tempted in the wilderness. Rabbi Lawrence Kushner offers us an image of the wilderness as not only a place but a possibility for renewal of soul:

> The wilderness is not just a desert through which we wandered for forty years. It is a way of being. A place that demands being open to the flow of life around you. A place that demands being honest with yourself without regard to the cost in personal anxiety. A place that demands being present with all of yourself. In the wilderness your possessions cannot surround you. Your preconceptions cannot protect you. Your logic cannot promise you the future. Your guilt can no longer place you safely in the past. You are left alone each day with an immediacy that astonishes, chastens, and exults. You see the world as if for the first time.[64]

The book of Numbers in Hebrew is called *B'midbar*, "In a Wilderness." In the Elder Testament, when people left their communities to go "into the wilderness," they were metaphorically going "into the word" or "into the essence of things." Paradoxically, the place of very few things (*midbar*, "wilderness") is the best place to contemplate the meaning of both our words and our things (*devarim*, "words," "things").

Entering the Land: Blessings and Curses—
Deuteronomy 27:12–13

When you have crossed over the Jordan,
these shall stand on Mount Gerizim for the blessing of the people:
Simeon, Levi, Judah, Issachar, Joseph, and Benjamin.
And these shall stand on Mount Ebal for the curse:
Reuben, Gad, Asher, Zebulun, Dan, and Naphtali.

When Abraham arrived in Canaan, he settled in the ancient village of Shechem, thirty miles north of Jerusalem and twenty miles west of the Jordan River (Gen. 12:6). Seven hundred years later when Moses ascended Mount Nebo, east of the river, he gazed upon a panoramic view of that very village in Canaan. Moses gave his blessing for Joshua to lead the people across the river into the land of Canaan, promised to them by God. This was the land they had struggled to reach for forty years. Moses would die on Mount Nebo at the age of 120.

After crossing the river, the families and livestock of the Israelites streamed through the small valley (today Shechem is the Palestinian city of Nablus in the West Bank). The village was flanked by two hills—Mount Gerizim to the south, and Mount Ebal to the north. Following God's direction, leaders of the twelve tribes stationed themselves atop the hills, six leaders representing six tribes on each hill. The Levites were instructed to shout a list of specific curses and blessings to the Israelites as they passed through the valley. Since the valley was narrow and the hills were low, the curses and blessings resonated through the natural amphitheater. Each blessed person answered, "Amen!" And each curse also received an "Amen!"

It's easy to understand why people would say "amen" to blessings, but why would God expect them to say "amen" to curses as well? A curse in modern Western culture is either a bad word—an expletive or obscenity—or an invocation to harm or jinx someone. The biblical idea of a curse, though, was what we would call a natural consequence of an action: "'Cursed be anyone who moves a neighbor's boundary marker.' All the people shall say, 'Amen!'" (Deut. 27:17). This is akin to saying there is a very serious consequence to anyone who moves a neighbor's boundary marker. In this context, the word *amen* is simply an affirmation of a statement. It literally means "truly," so it is often spoken to express the sentiment, "That's the truth!"

It must have been extraordinary to see tens of thousands of people walking in the midst of shouts of curses and blessings from the Levites, then calling back one "Amen!" after another. Think about how you respond to the blessings and curses in your life. Whether we say it aloud or not, or are even aware of it, we too must say "Amen!" to both the positive and negative consequences of our actions. This ritual mass chorus of "amens" was a fitting way to end the forty-year Exodus journey for the Hebrews, and it serves as a strong reminder for us to affirm life— all of life.

A Prophet in Israel Like Moses—
Deuteronomy 34:10–11

Never since has there arisen a prophet in Israel like Moses, whom the LORD
knew face to face. He was unequaled for all the signs and wonders that the
LORD sent him to perform in the land of Egypt.

Jews call Moses *Moshe Rabbeinu,* or "Moses our Teacher," a title
that reflects his ongoing inspiration to the Jewish people in every
generation. We read of Moses from the time he was a baby on the Nile
through standing atop Mount Nebo overlooking Canaan at 120, about to
die. Yet, what do we really know about Moses? In a creative and original
biographical study called *Moses: A Stranger among Us,* Rabbi Maurice Harris
challenges the typical view we have of Moses as an insider, and asks us
to consider him as a model for people of faith who are struggling within
their own religious traditions:

> In the Jewish world, Moses is usually described as the
> consummate *insider* of our tradition because of his close
> relationship with God. . . . But the Torah goes to great lengths
> to show us in Moses a man who actually lived most of his
> life as an *outsider* to the Israelites. . . . His upbringing in the
> Pharaoh's court, his marriage to a non-Israelite woman, and
> even his failure to set foot in the sacred land of his people
> all place him at the margins of the Israelite community.
> Moses is, in fact, both an outsider and an insider—something
> that makes him surprisingly relevant to the many Jews and
> Christians today who find themselves simultaneously drawn
> to and uncomfortable with their faith traditions.[65]

Raised as an adopted son of Pharaoh's daughter Batya, the Princess of Egypt, he became God's ambassador to lead the Hebrews out of slavery, and teach them to fulfill the commandments they received at Sinai. He traveled with them for forty years in the wilderness and put up with their idol worship of the golden calf, their incessant complaining about food and water, and their lack of confidence in the face of the challenges ahead. Through it all, Moses is the paradigm of patience and compassion. His intercessory prayer, pleading with God on the people's behalf, is bold, creative, and illuminating.

Moses loved the nation of newly emancipated slaves who followed him into the wilderness on their way to the unfamiliar home of their ancestors. They crossed the Red Sea with him, battled Amalek by his side, received the Ten Commandments with him, and committed themselves to an everlasting covenant with God—all on blind faith. He understood that as slaves they had little education and their will to fight had been broken. But Moses also knew that their souls were on fire to bring the God of their ancestors back into their lives.

The world has been inspired by the brilliant oratory of Moses, especially his words in the book of Deuteronomy. In the final months of his life, he gave three major discourses, chanted a spectacular song (known as the "Song of Moses"), and gave personalized blessings to each of the tribes. His words were designed to ensure the survival of the young and emerging nation. When we read them now, knowing he was soon to die, it touches our hearts; knowing the backstory of his remarkable life, it moves our souls.

At the end of Deuteronomy, the 120-year-old Moses has already seen his sister Miriam and brother Aaron die, along with all the old-timers from his generation. He stands atop Mount Nebo looking into Canaan when God says to him, "This is the land of which I swore to Abraham, to Isaac, and to Jacob, saying, 'I will give it to your descendants'; I have let you see it with your eyes, but you shall not cross over there" (Deut. 34:4).

Reading the text, or hearing it chanted aloud in a synagogue each year, we feel the poignancy and pathos of this moment not because he will die—at 120 this is to be expected—but because after all he has endured, he will only glimpse the Promised Land. We want to plead with God on his behalf: *With all that he went through, please God, let Moses, your beloved servant, enter the Land.* But he dies and is buried nearby, having only glimpsed the Promised Land from afar. Many of us weep when we hear the final verses of Deuteronomy chanted in synagogues each autumn.

It might be natural to think, *If Moses couldn't get to the Promised Land, what hope is there for me?* But most of us know we will have some unfulfilled dreams at the end of life, whether it be projects not completed or relationships unresolved. The commentary that Moses died in peace despite his final wish not being fulfilled ironically gives us hope. Perhaps in our last days we may think, *If Moshe Rabbeinu couldn't achieve all he wanted in life, I can release the anxiety I carry for not achieving all of my dreams.*

The lesson in the story of Moses's death naturally transfers to the crucifixion story. Does the crucifixion of Jesus make a Christian hopeless? Certainly not. The crucifixion leads to the resurrection, and the resurrection leads to the remission of sin. What looks like a failure ultimately leads to redemption. Neither the life of Moses nor the life of Jesus ends at their death. Rather, their deaths are part of larger, ongoing stories. For Jews, the death of Moses is the beginning of a nation and what will eventually become the nation of Israel and the Jewish religion.

Just as the story of resurrection is constantly inspiring and transformational in Christianity, the Exodus story continually lives in the hearts of the Jews: "Never since has there arisen a prophet in Israel like Moses, whom the LORD knew face to face. He was unequaled for all the signs and wonders that the LORD sent him to perform in the land of Egypt." The story of Moses's courage is our template of rising from bondage and cleaving to God. The journey of the Exodus continues to be told by the Jewish people to the whole world, from generation to generation. It is the most influential and inspiring liberation story ever told.

PART THREE

A Matrix—
Exodus and the Cross

Springtime Festivals: Passover and Easter

To Christians, the story of Jesus's life, death, and resurrection echoes the Exodus story of the Jewish people. As the blood of the Passover lamb protected the ancient Jewish people from the angel of death, so the blood of Jesus protects every Christian from the spiritual death that comes from sin. As the Hebrews are liberated from physical enslavement, so the Christian is liberated from spiritual enslavement to sin by the blood of the Paschal sacrifice—the crucified Jesus. The Jewish and Christian stories are different, but clearly parallel and analogous. The Christian story does not complete or replace the Jewish story—it is a rendering of the original story, applied to sin.

As Communion is a reenactment of Christ's death and resurrection that brings redemption, the Passover seder meal in every Jewish home is a reenactment of redemption and liberation from enslavement. The Jewish and Christian stories are complementary; both are told each spring in the midst of the renewal and rebirth of nature itself. The Jewish story of liberation and the Christian story of resurrection are both rooted in God's image embedded and reflected in nature. This yearly renewal in nature is the template.

Passover, Easter, *Shavuot,* and Pentecost are all built upon earlier festivals of ancient cultures in the Near East. As mentioned earlier, the Jewish Passover is built upon the foundation of ancient farming and shepherd festivals held every spring. Fifty days later a second festival celebrated the early summer wheat harvest. Despite the stereotype of pre-monotheistic people as idolatrous heathens, they invented farming, ranching, writing, property rights, cities, and the earliest law codes—elements that form the foundation of Western civilization.

Enslavement and death, liberation and resurrection. Two stories for two faiths to tell and retell in every generation, for each individual to experience in their own story of faith. The Jew is to experience a personal liberation from the elements in the world that are pharaonic and enslaving. The Christian is to experience the renewal that comes from being freed from sin and forgiven of personal iniquities.

Just as I searched for the beginning of the Exodus story, I now search for the beginning of the Easter story. Does it begin with the crucifixion? Or five days before on Palm Sunday? Maybe the Easter story really begins years earlier when Jesus is preaching the Gospel? Or maybe at his birth. Or before his birth when Mary is told by the angel Gabriel that she is to give birth to a son and name him Jesus. Could it be that the Easter story really begins in the prophecies of the Elder Testament that foretell the future Messiah? Once again, here is the dilemma. Is there really a point in time at which the Easter story begins? Just like the Passover story for Jews, we can also trace the origin of the Easter story to the first words of Genesis. The Gospel of John begins with a recapitulation of the Creation story. In John 1:1–5, he writes:

> In the beginning was the Word, and the Word was with God, and the Word was God. He was in the beginning with God. All things came into being through him, and without him not one thing came into being. What has come into being in him was life, and the life was the light of all people. The light shines in the darkness, and the darkness did not overcome it.

John's insight parallels Jewish theology. What is the Word, the Logos, in Christianity? Jesus. What is the Word, the Logos, in Judaism? Torah. Jesus and Torah are not one and the same, but they are *yakhdav*, one in purpose. If, as previously suggested, we think of the creation of the cosmos as the original model for the Passover story—as God's own self-liberation from the empty void into the Promised Land of existence—then in Christianity we might think of it as the original model for the Easter story—as God's own self-resurrection from the empty void into the promise of salvation.

The Afterlife of Events

When Jews gather each year for the Passover seder, the story is told of the Holy One redeeming their ancestors from Egypt with these words, "We were slaves to Pharaoh in Egypt but God took us out of there with a mighty hand and an outstretched arm." At the beautifully decorated seder table with all its symbolic foods, Jews create an atmosphere that transcends time. By performing this ancient home ritual, it's as if each Jewish family is taking a journey back in time. Biblical scholar Rabbi Irving Greenberg gives us a way to understand the importance of the Exodus as a story that transcends time:

> The secret of the impact of the Exodus is that it does not present itself as ancient history, a one-time event. Since the key way to remember the Exodus is reenactment, the event offers itself as an ongoing experience in human history. As free people relive the Exodus, it turns memory into moral dynamic. . . . The past is not excised but becomes an active part of the lives of the participants.[66]

Every year at seders throughout the world, Jews read aloud the words "God redeemed us with them." At that moment the transtemporal power of the entire seder ritual becomes evident. The past transports itself into the present—a state of mind called anamnesis. In the Haggadah, family members read aloud these words by the first-century sage Rabbi Gamaliel:

> In each generation, a man must regard himself as if he came forth himself out of Egypt, as it is said, "You shall tell your children on that day, saying, 'It is because of what God did for me when I went free out of Egypt.' For the Holy One redeemed

not only our ancestors, God redeemed us with them, as it is said, 'God took us out of there to bring us to the land that God promised to our ancestors.'" [67]

The function of the yearly retelling of the Exodus story on Passover is to make the past come alive. The simple practice of remembrance is central to understanding what the Exodus story has meant to Jews throughout the ages, and how it led to the rebirth of the state of Israel in May 1948, after almost 2,000 years of exile. Dr. Robert Louis Wilken, professor of Christianity at the University of Virginia, writes about the parallel ways Jews and Christians understand the practice of remembrance in their rituals. Commenting on the words of Rabbi Gamaliel in the Haggadah, Dr. Wilken writes:

> Here "remembrance" is not simple recall. The person who celebrates *Pesakh* [Passover] is not a distant spectator. He or she is a participant, for what happened then is now being represented in the Seder. As Gamaliel says, "It is I who came forth out of Egypt." What God did in the past, he continues to do in the present, not in a general way, but through the Seder ritual. [68]

The language of "what God did for me" and "God redeemed us with them" leaps off the page of the Haggadah, and makes the redemption of an enslaved people more than 3,300 years ago the key to understanding our own lives. We are inspired to ask: Where am I enslaved? Who is the pharaoh in my life? From where will my redemption come? Christian ritual offers the same kind of anamnesis in the experience of the Easter resurrection through the Eucharist. Dr. Lawrence Hoffman, professor of liturgy at Hebrew Union College, writes:

> When Jesus says of bread and wine, "in remembrance of me," he means the same thing that Jewish tradition does when it calls

bread "a remembrance of [or pointer to] the paschal lamb." Eating it will point to Jesus, who, like the paschal sacrifice, reenacts the original lamb's slaughter and points God's ways toward merciful redemption.[69]

Dr. Marek Tamm, professor of cultural history at Tallinn University in Estonia, calls this remembrance ritual the "afterlife of events." The historical Passover and Easter are long over, but they live on in the spiritual present tense—an afterlife beyond the restraints of linear time. In both Judaism and Christianity, these are not sentimental memories of grand redemptive events that took place in the past. Nor can they simply be dismissed as sacred myths. During Passover and Easter, the Exodus and the Resurrection become present-tense events for believers.

Bible scholar Dr. Pamela Barmash explains how the retelling of the Exodus story each year helps bring the past back to life:

> Exodus is the past made present. It is not an event of mere antiquarian interest. Rather, it is a symbolic representation of distant past as both embedded and mirrored in contemporary reality and action. The Exodus may be grounded in the past, but it is experienced in the present. When Jews remember the Exodus, they feel that they are part of a collective, a group continuing throughout time. They link their history to their remote ancestors and reaffirm their standing as part of a historical people extending through time. . . . The Exodus enables Jews to see beyond the limits of their contemporary existence by utilizing the past to lay claim to the future.[70]

This idea of an afterlife of events is what Dr. Michael Walzer, in his book *Exodus and Revolution*, refers to as "eternal recurrence":

> A political history with a strong linearity, a strong forward movement, the Exodus gives permanent shape to Jewish

conceptions of time; and it serves as a model, ultimately, for non-Jewish conceptions too. We can think of it as the crucial alternative to all mythic notions of eternal recurrence—and hence to those cyclical understandings of political change from which our word 'revolution' derives. The idea of eternal recurrence connects the social to the natural world and gives to political life the simple closure of a circle: birth, maturity, death, and rebirth.[71]

To the mystics in all religions, an authentic revelation is eternal and not bound by the natural laws of time and space. The seder is not merely symbolic of the redemption but a reenactment of it on a spiritual level. For Christians too the Eucharist is not just lovely symbolism, but a spiritual reality empowering the participant to partake of the mystery of the resurrection.

Rabbi Mordechai HaKohen, a sixteenth-century kabbalist, offers us this gem of wisdom: "Once the Torah was given it became timeless and cut loose from any one place: every moment is its moment and every place its place."[72] One can sense this is precisely how, in Philippians 3:10–11, Paul wanted to understand the Resurrection, not as a past event, but as an ongoing process within his own life: "I want to know Christ and the power of his resurrection and the sharing of his sufferings by becoming like him in his death, if somehow I may attain the resurrection from the dead."

As mentioned earlier, every Friday evening when Jewish families welcome the Sabbath by sanctifying wine with a prayer called kiddush they are giving an "afterlife" to two events, the Creation and the Exodus. Why? The Exodus reminds us that even when things are going well, circumstances can change and life can take unexpected, painful turns. But it is hyperlinked to the Creation. When things are going badly, there will be a reset, a chance for a new beginning. That's why we also remember "the workings of creation." Since God is continually creating the world, we too are continually being created and re-created.

Although Jews don't generally use the word *sacrament*, kiddush has a sacramental function—setting something (wine) apart so that we can experience what it represents. The function of chanting kiddush is similar to Augustine's teaching that a sacrament is a visible form of an invisible grace. The grace is pressing the reset button of creation and getting an automatic renewal in the Sabbath—that each time we get stuck in one of life's Egypts, there will be a liberation, and then a new beginning. With patience and faith, our negative experiences can be transformed into positives. As King David chanted, "You have turned my mourning into dancing" (Ps. 30:11).

Dr. Wilken draws a direct link between kiddush and Christian Eucharist in the understanding of sacrifice:

> In a sacrament, a spiritual reality is conveyed through a material object. . . . In the Christian Eucharist, the bread and wine are visible forms that convey an invisible blessing. What one sees is bread and wine, but what one receives is Christ. . . . The language of sacrifice comes directly out of Jewish tradition, and the prominence of a term such as "lamb of God . . . " has broad symbolic links to Jewish practices at the time of the Christian beginnings. In calling the Eucharist a sacrifice, Christians wish to say that their liturgy is not a memorial meal recalling what happened centuries ago, but a re-presenting of what happened once for the benefit of the present community. . . . In the Christian liturgy, the term "remembrance" means re-presenting, re-actualizing, making present what happened in the past.[73]

Nobel Prize-winning author and teacher Elie Wiesel said memory is intrinsic to being Jewish. Look at the way the Holocaust is remembered. One of the universal gifts of Judaism is for all people who have suffered injustice to have the Exodus story, whose lessons can be applied to their own lives. Elie Wiesel's understanding of the past as a living present is not a Jewish idea. The same is true for Christianity in applying the lessons of the Crucifixion to understanding human suffering. Universal spiritual experiences echo in the Exodus and Crucifixion stories, and the sacred practice of remembering has profound value for anyone who has endured catastrophe. The wisdom from Elie Wiesel's Nobel acceptance speech on December 10, 1986, is just as important as it was in the past:

> Without memory, our existence would be barren and opaque, like a prison cell into which no light penetrates; like a tomb which rejects the living. . . . For me, hope without memory is like memory without hope. . . . The opposite of the past is not the future but the absence of future; the opposite of the future is not the past but the absence of past. The loss of one is equivalent to the sacrifice of the other. For us, forgetting was never an option. Remembering is a noble and necessary act. The call of memory, the call to memory, reaches us from the very dawn of history. No commandment figures so frequently, so insistently, in the Bible. It is incumbent upon us to remember the good we have received, and the evil we have suffered.[74]

The Rhythm of Life

The Passover and Easter festivals are both rooted in nature. Liberation and resurrection are themes that emerge from what is happening every spring. A fascinating aspect of Creation is that in temperate climates it's the winter that actually makes the renewal of spring possible. After the cold and rainy season, when the weather gets warmer, the shells around the seeds begin to crack. It's the decay of the shell that once protected the seeds that allows the shoots to arise. This is all analogous to the underlying meaning of the Exodus and the Cross—both represent the transformation of winter's sleep into the new life of spring.

The Passion, death, and resurrection of Jesus becomes the template through which Christians see themselves: they can see the hope of rebirth arising from the soil of their own suffering. Communion can be thought of as a fractal of nature itself. The consumption of the body and blood of Christ makes sense when understood in terms of this metaphor of nature. Whether one views it symbolically or literally, as consubstantiation or as transubstantiation, when Christians partake in the Eucharist, it is not an empty ritual, but a reenactment of Creation. In a way, the act of eating is, or ought to be, an act of communion.

Dr. Kalman Bland, professor emeritus from Duke University, uses the metaphor of music in an amazing way to explore the awesome and terrifying nature of Passover's death and life themes:

> Passover is polyphonic. Its melodies are contrapuntal. Although the tonality of bliss prevails, bereavement and solemnity compete for attention. Passover's harmonies are equally complex. A palimpsest of unmistakably audible layers, Passover combines the Allegro Vivace of major keys with the Lacrimoso of minor chords. The joyous festival celebrating redemption and spring

simultaneously commemorates death. The commemoration of mortality, in all of its dimensions, vibrates with multiple strains. The sweet mingles with the bitter. The unbridled satisfactions of hoping for and witnessing the undoing of hateful oppressors blends with the grief of mourning the demise of beloved victims. Passover can be terrifying.[75]

We live within this terrifying dichotomy, in a pulsing world of duality of rhythmic contractions and expansions, ins and outs, highs and lows, moments of sadness and moments of joy. We see it in our breathing, the beating of our hearts, and digestion. Oxygen in, carbon dioxide out. Food in, waste out. Addressing God as the pulsing Breath of Life, Rabbi Arthur Waskow brings to life the deeper meaning of what is called the Tetragrammaton, the four-letter name of God (YHVH) generally translated as "Lord." The Hebrew word is derived from the verb for "being." Rabbi Waskow suggests that the name might have originally been the divine appellation referring to actual sounds made when breathing:

> You are the breathing that gives life to all the worlds.
> And we do the breathing that gives life to all the worlds.
> As we breathe out what the trees breathe in.
> And the trees breathe out what we breathe in,
> So we breathe each other into life.
> We and You.
> *YyyyHhhhWwwwHhhh.*[76]

There is a holy poetry in the rhythm of life we experience as duality. In physics we see the interaction of oppositional forces that are part of a greater singularity in the wave-particle duality. In biology, we see animal waste resulting in nitrogen-fixing bacteria that fertilize the soil. These dichotomies are divinely installed in the operating systems of every natural science, and celebrated in the seasons that religions commemorate with festivals and holy convocations: autumn for thanksgiving and springtime for renewal, and in the winter—celebrations of the light during the darkest days of the year. In this world of duality, the only true singularity is God. "*YHVH echad,*" the Hebrew in Deuteronomy 6:4 means, "the LORD is one." Recognition of that oneness is what the Israelites experienced fifty days into their Exodus journey on Mount Sinai, commemorated each year during the festival of Shavuot, fifty days after every Passover.

By the mere fact of being created, the creation is no longer a part of its Creator. Duality comes into existence the very moment of birth and creation, analogous to the relationship of a newborn to its mother. The world emerges from the oneness of God. Our religions are our poetic and noble attempts to get as close as we can to that Oneness. In Judaism, the soul of each person is understood to be a spark of God, just as Christians see the indwelling Holy Spirit. The faithful experience a sense of oneness with the Divine, yet can never be fully at one with God. It is that internal spark, the Holy Spirit, that Jews and Christians respectively seek to encounter through spiritual practices and rituals. Retelling the Exodus story every Passover serves to get the Jewish people as close to oneness as possible by celebrating the miracle of every spring. Christianity, likewise, has the same goal in the telling of the Passion story.

As created beings we look at God's oneness as outsiders, hopefully as close outsiders, like children to a parent. In our various denominations, we often name God with terms of relationship: Father, Mother, Beloved, Friend. We pray, thank, and petition the One, but we innately know that we are not at one with the One. Yet, for a few brief moments during prayer and meditation, we can experience our essence—the spark of the divine within us, our soul. During moments of ecstatic joy, or even deep grief, we are given glimpses of that oneness. We feel we are speaking to and contemplating a Oneness—the Holy One of Being that we are intimately related to. The seeker and lover of God has that one aim: to recognize, greet, and give thanks to that intrinsic Unity that lies beneath the surface of all creation, beneath the apparent dichotomy and duality.

In yachting, the sail turned at an angle transforms the force of the wind blowing into the sailor's face into a wind at the sailor's back. This permits the boat to "miraculously" travel windward. Isn't that an apt metaphor for the interdependent nature of oppositional forces? Even in the face of the forces of sadness and loss, the Holy One transforms our loss into gain, and we travel windward against the losses in our lives. As the Christian mystic, poet, and artist William Blake reminds us in *Auguries of Innocence*:

> Joy and woe are woven fine,
> A clothing for the soul divine;
> Under every grief and pine
> Runs a joy with silken twine.
> It is right it should be so,
> We were made for joy and woe,
> And when this we rightly know,
> Through the world we safely go.

Jews celebrate Passover in the spring, around the time that Christians celebrate Easter, and it is the dual aspects of slavery and freedom in Judaism, and death and resurrection in Christianity, that each faith tries to reconcile. In our emotional lives, the dichotomy of opposite feelings actually enriches our lives. None of us wants to be sad, but we know we will have times in our lives when we are down. And it is those down times that enable us to appreciate life when we are joyous. None of us want to be ill, but the return to health after sickness can be exhilarating. Our losses permit us to appreciate our gains. Our disappointments give us the ability to recognize our successes. And so too does death enable us to love and appreciate life. These too are part of the rhythm of life.

Easter commemorates the death of the Christian Messiah on Good Friday and culminates in his resurrection on Sunday, becoming a paradigm for personal rebirth. The Easter story continues from Jesus, the individual, and extends outward to the body of the church. The

Passover story starts with Israel, the nation, and moves inward to every individual. Slavery and freedom, death and resurrection are the themes of the springtime festivals of Judaism and Christianity. The rhythmic duality of death and life in nature are the focal points for describing a rhythmic balance echoed in both faiths each spring.

Broad Way, Narrow Way

We can frame the contrast between Exodus and the Cross metaphorically as the broad way and narrow way. The Christian's path is the narrow way of Jesus: "Enter through the narrow gate" (Matt. 7:13). The path for the Jew, on the other hand, is the broad way: "Your commandment is exceedingly broad" (Ps. 119:96). While both are stories of liberation, the focal point of each is different.

The traditional Christian view starts with Jesus's suffering on the cross. From that sacred, narrow focal point, the believer is then able to grasp and empathize with all suffering. In the traditional Christian view, atonement is achieved through Jesus's death and resurrection, though not all Christians subscribe to this notion of substitutionary atonement.

The Jew begins by retelling the Exodus story and the suffering in slavery of the entire Hebrew people. By being part of a broad group and participating in its suffering, each individual can then understand the suffering of every child, every martyr, and the helpless of every nation. From this broad view, substitutionary atonement applies to everyone who suffers.

Jews and Christians achieve spiritual liberation but from opposite directions. For a Christian, everyone's suffering points back to Jesus's suffering, and the liberation from personal sin that evokes empathy for the world. For the Jew, Jesus's suffering is the suffering of one more Jew whose pain and passion is no greater than the suffering of anyone else. For the Christian, Jesus's suffering encompasses the suffering of all of humanity. The Jew sees everyone as a son or daughter of God, all yearning for freedom from oppression. The Christian's starting point is with Jesus who is seen as God's son. The Jew begins with the entire nation of Israel as the firstborn son. As God says to Moses: "Thus says the LORD: Israel is my firstborn son" (Exod. 4:22).

Walking the narrow way, some Christians see God's incarnation as belonging solely to Jesus. Jewish mystics describe the incarnation of God in a concept called *hitgashmut*, meaning that which takes on physical form broadened to include God's voice, angels, the Torah, and the spark of the divine in everyone. To the Jew the focus is not upon twelve disciples but upon twelve tribes of people. Likewise, Jews have a broadened view of mediation and redemptive suffering. To a Jew there are many mediators, many intermediaries to help the believer reach God. Both systems obviously work—how else could they have survived for thousands of years and made such great contributions to the flowering of humanity? Dr. Martin Buber's commentary on a Hasidic teaching supports this idea:

> This is the secret of the unity of God. No matter where I take hold of a shred of it, I hold the whole of it. And since the teachings, and also the *mitzvot*, are radiations of His being, he who lovingly does one *mitzvah* utterly, and to the core, and in this one *mitzvah* takes hold of a shred of the unity of God, holds the whole of it in his hand, and has fulfilled all.[77]

Tohubohu: Creation, Passover, and Easter

Both the Exodus story and the resurrection are rooted in the Creation story in Genesis. The three stories are different—each is unique—but under the surface all are related. The second line in Genesis tells us that moments before creation, "the earth was without form, and void" (Gen. 1:2, KJV). The King James Bible's translations "without form" and "void" come from the Hebrew words *tohu* and *vohu*, which have been imported into English as the blended word *tohubohu*. Etymologists are uncertain of the original meanings of the Hebrew words, and they perplexed translators even in Jesus's lifetime, but exploring them will yield some helpful insights about the Creation, Passover, and Easter.

Judaica Press translates the words together as "astonishingly empty." This interpretive translation goes back 2,000 years to a brilliant Judean scholar named Onkelos, who lived in the generation just after Jesus. In Hebrew this pair of words form an alliterative rhyme, and they use a common biblical device whereby doubling a word adds emphasis or creates a sense of the superlative (e.g., holy of holies, song of songs, servant of servants, etc.). *Tohu* and *vohu* are usually translated in English as somewhat synonymous (i.e., empty and void, unformed and desolate), but in Hebrew they are possibly an expression of some preexistent duality. Even though "without form" is the binary opposite of "form," ancient Hebrew might have been trying to express a kind of internal opposition within formlessness—*tohu* and *vohu*.

The Hebrew implies that *tohu* is nonbeing in a relaxed, soft state, whereas *vohu* is nonbeing in a contracted state. Think of a baseball pitcher winding up before the pitch. First the arm is relaxed and soft (*tohu*), and then comes the wind up. The arm is arched and wound up behind the shoulder (*vohu*), but the ball has still not been thrown. Then in an instant the toss of the ball becomes "In the beginning"—the creation. Nonbeing comes into being. Creation *ex nihilo*. *Tohu* and *vohu* might also be described in what physics calls potential and kinetic energy. *Tohu* is the potential, and *vohu* is the kinetic energy in motion before it fully is expressed. The great sixteenth-century Italian scholar Obadja Sforno had a similar sense when he said that *tohu* is potential at rest whereas *vohu* is potential in motion and on its way to becoming real.

In biblical Hebrew, Creation is not a past-tense event; it is continuous, ongoing in every moment. The DNA of the Passover and Easter originate in the pattern of the Creation. *Tohu* is the contraction, the primal exile. *Vohu* is the expansion, the primal redemption. The Creation story is the primal revelation—the revealing of energy transformed into matter, of nonbeing transformed into being. We may love to study the Creation in our Bible classes and see how it is analogous to events in physics, cosmology, and evolutionary biology, but it's an abstract, intellectual story that inspires awe but doesn't really touch the heart until we see how it affects the lives of real people. That's where Passover and Easter come in. We can study the relationship between the heavens and the earth intellectually, but we can personally relate to the enslavement of the Jews or the crucifixion of Jesus. The Passover and Easter stories are Creation made personal.

In my previous book, *Jesus: First-Century Rabbi*,[78] I shared how the Passover story sums up the Jewish concepts of exile, redemption, and revelation. The exile was enslavement, redemption was the liberation, and revelation was the receiving of the Torah fifty days after the slaves were freed. In Hebrew, all three words, *exile, redemption,* and *revelation,* come from the same two-letter root, *gimmel lamed,* which has to do with a wheel rolling and turning in a forward direction—exile, redemption, and revelation *roll* from one to the next.

When I told this to my colleague Rev. Anne Bartlett, an Episcopal priest, she immediately recognized the underlying rolling pattern as it is expressed in the Easter story. Good Friday, the day of the crucifixion, is comparable to exile. Easter Sunday, the day of resurrection, is comparable to the redemption. And fifty days later, Pentecost, the arrival of the Holy Spirit, is the revelation. Just as Jews count fifty days from Passover to

Shavuot when God revealed the Torah at Sinai, so Christians count fifty days to Pentecost when the Holy Spirit descended upon the apostles and other followers of Jesus. The connection between Judaism and Christianity is clear: exile and crucifixion, liberation and resurrection, revelation of Torah and revelation of the Holy Spirit. Two stories for two religions, yet both with a common DNA derived from the Creation. These two stories for two different covenantal missions seem to be harmonized by God to each other.

Exile, redemption, and revelation. In the telling of the Passover story these three theological concepts can be summarized very simply: we were enslaved, we were freed, we found out why. Isn't that the pattern that we've each seen in our own lives? We get "enslaved" and stuck in some miserable situation, so we struggle for freedom. We get delivered and liberated, but we still don't know why we suffered. With a little patience, in an emblematic fifty days, and a lot of prayer, we find out why we suffered, and what benefit might possibly come from our pain.

The pattern is there in Christianity as well. The center of the Easter story is not the crucifixion. That's just the beginning. The crucifixion is the exile, the contraction, potential energy, *tohu*. The real power comes in the resurrection, the redemption, expansion, *vohu*, the kinetic energy of Easter. But just as Jesus's family and disciples were mystified as to why he had to die, it took fifty days until the Holy Spirit descended—with that came the revelation, the focal point of all that kinetic energy. As different as the Passover story for Jews and the Easter story for Christians may be, they are fractals of one another.

Passover is the story of the liberation of an entire people. Easter is the story of the resurrection of a single man. But they both share the same chromosomal double helix: death and life. Both are interpreted to apply to the individual lives of the faithful of each religion. As a Jew I do not apply the story of Jesus to my life, but I can witness and celebrate the application of Jesus's death and resurrection when I see how essential it is to the life of Christians. My Christian friends, on the other hand, have utilized the Passover story and applied it to their own lives and to hundreds of liberation struggles throughout the ages. To that we raise our cups and say, *"L'chaim*—to life!"

Redemption: The Spiritual Cost of Freedom

What is redemption? What does it mean when we say that the liberation of the Israelite slaves was an act of redemption on the part of God? In Exodus 6:6–7, God says:

> Say therefore to the Israelites, 'I am the LORD, and I will free you from the burdens of the Egyptians and deliver you from slavery to them. I will redeem you with an outstretched arm and with mighty acts of judgment. I will take you as my people, and I will be your God.

There is a spiritual principle espoused by many religions, expressed by using the metaphor of commerce: for all human actions there are costs and gains. The gain of freedom is paid for with the cost of redemptive acts. For example, when God redeems the children of Israel, the cost will be adherence to a covenant—to maintain high standards of belief and conduct as outlined in the Torah as *mitzvot* (commandments). For many Christians, the gain of freedom from sin is seen to be paid for with the suffering of Jesus. Here are a few examples of covenantal obligations the Israelites agreed to follow during the Exodus in "repayment" for their redemption:

> **Knowing that God is faithful:** The LORD has brought you out with a mighty hand, and redeemed you from the house of slavery. . . . Know therefore that the LORD your God is God, the faithful God who maintains covenant loyalty with those who love him and keep his commandments. (Deut. 7:8–9)

Generosity upon releasing servants: Provide liberally out of your flock . . . thus giving to him some of the bounty with which the LORD your God has blessed you. Remember that you were a slave in the land of Egypt, and the LORD your God redeemed you. (Deut. 15:14–15)

Justice for the vulnerable: You shall not deprive a resident alien or an orphan of justice; you shall not take a widow's garment in pledge. Remember that you were a slave in Egypt and the LORD your God redeemed you from there. (Deut. 24:17–18)

In Hebrew the accumulation of gains accrued from the performance of *mitzvot* is called *zekhut*, "merit." When Abraham was commanded to offer his son Isaac, his faith in God is known as *zekhut Yitzhak*, the "merit of Isaac." The Jewish people "cash in" (redeem) this merit every Rosh Hashanah, the Jewish New Year, and get forgiveness in return. The *shofar* (ram's horn) is blown as a reminder of both the near-sacrifice of Isaac and the actual sacrifice of the ram as the one that carries away the sins of the people.

The word *redemption* comes from the Middle English "to buy back." The same sense of trade or economic exchange is in the biblical Hebrew word *g'ulah*, which can mean "ransom, redeem by payment." Most Jews and Christians don't have a clear idea about what redemption really means. The best analogy I can think of (I realize it's somewhat trivial) has to do with the way we use the word *redeem* in reference to grocery coupons. The shopper clips the coupon and redeems it for a discount— this piece of paper representing someone's action is exchanged for the reduction in cost. Redemption implies exchanging one thing for another—suffering for joy, struggle for freedom, death for life.

Redemption is also a theological metaphor that arises out of nature. Exchange of energy is at the center of chemistry, physics, biology, and cosmology. Life and death are so intertwined that most of us are not even aware of the exchange between the living and the dead. If you compost, you are participating in the Creator's process of converting once-living fruits and vegetables into soil that we describe as "alive" with nutrients. The decay and "death" of organic material becomes rich soil and fertilizer. Manure is waste, yet out of it come nitrogen-fixing bacteria that enrich our gardens. The word *humus*, from the Latin for "ground," is a cognate with *human*. In the Hebrew, the etymology reflects the same meaning. Adam's name means "human" and derives from *adamah*, which means "earth." There is a real energetic exchange between the organic and the inorganic world, between humans and the planet. Something is exchanged for something else.

The explicit understanding of redemption in the Bible is that everything has a cost: in physical terms (e.g., redeeming a captive for money); in social justice terms (e.g., redeeming a nation from bondage); in familial terms (e.g., redeeming the death of a brother; see Deut. 25:5–10); or in spiritual terms (e.g., God redeeming the Israelites from slavery; Jesus's death redeeming Christians from sin). The theological concept of redemption can be compared to the principle of *karma* that is central to Hinduism and Buddhism.

But why, the sensitive seeker must ask, does God ask Abraham to offer his son? Why does God require the plagues and the death of the firstborn Egyptians for the Hebrews to be redeemed? Why does God require Jesus to die on the cross for Christians to be redeemed from sin? It is difficult for the modern mind to grasp the theological meaning of this kind of exchange. It has, in fact, been misused by religious leaders who conflate suffering with divine punishment and blame victims for bringing about their own suffering. The notion of something good coming out of suffering also goes against our cultural sense of fairness. When we hear of a tragedy and say, "That isn't fair," we are right. We are right to ask why a loving God permits the innocent to suffer. Is there any answer to this theological question that doesn't sound glib and simplistic?

Part of the mystery of the natural world is that pain and death are built into the code of creation. The Creator has set in motion a world with incalculable devastation through what we call "natural disasters," with rampant violence between predator and prey. Imagine this scene from a nature documentary: a jaguar has killed an antelope; in the same frame, lions are surrounding the kill site using a group strategy to steal the carcass from the jaguar; in the background, the viewer hears the haunting cackle of hyenas avariciously circling this arena of life and death. Regardless of how much the jaguar, lions, and hyenas eventually consume of the antelope, the devastating process of rot and decay would ultimately consume every remaining cell of flesh and bone.

We consider this kind of devastation and violence part of "nature" but unacceptable in human nature. In the world of humans, such acts are, thank God, classified as immoral and criminal. Yet we still face the reality that God has established a system whereby the innocent die from natural disaster and disease, and in wars they did not start. How can we justify such suffering in our theologies? (See the appendix "Theodicy: Divine Providence & the Existence of Evil" on pages 204–215 for more on this.) Is there a lesson to be learned from the Jewish and Christian redemption stories of the Exodus and the Cross that can help us make sense of tragic suffering? The observance of Passover for Jews and Easter for Christians prompts the participant to reflect on the meaning of the suffering in the stories of slavery and crucifixion. This, in turn, inspires self-reflection and *teshuvah*, a desire to repent and return to God.

Repentance helps bring about a degree of redemption. Why? Because there is, so to speak, some leftover energy from the courage it took for the person to repent. God applies this leftover energy to the "account" of the sins of the whole world. Rabbi Yonanan said, "Great is repentance, for it brings redemption, as it is said, 'A redeemer will come to Zion, and unto them that turn from transgression in Jacob'" (Isa. 59:20).[79]

On Good Friday, the Christian grieves when contemplating the suffering and crucifixion of Jesus. Every Jew grieves when hearing of the binding of Isaac, the death of Aaron's sons, or the death of Egypt's firstborn sons. This grieving creates an internal, psychological transformation. It inspires empathy for anyone who is suffering, and that empathy brings about atonement. As recorded in the Talmud (Sanhedrin 101a), Rabbi Akiva, who was born very soon after Jesus was crucified, taught, "Suffering is precious." How is this possible? The footnote in the Talmud explains, "It makes atonement for the sufferer."[80] Like Jesus and thousands of other Jewish martyrs, Rabbi Akiva too was tortured to death by the Romans in 136 CE for teaching Judaism in defiance of Hadrian's edict against the Jews.

Every Christian must ask: Why did Jesus have to die? And every Jew must ask: Why did Akiva have to die? Why did innocent Egyptian firstborn sons have to die? Why does any innocent person have to suffer? And no matter what any rabbi, pastor, or priest may tell us, there is no satisfactory answer except that redemption has a cost and that suffering has meaning. We may accumulate *zekhut*, merit, for our good deeds. We may even draw upon the *zekhut* of others when we are suffering, but the ledger in heaven always has to balance at some point.

The theological epicenter of Judaism revolves around the Exodus, which leads to the core Jewish value of moral responsibility. The master story in Christianity centers on the crucifixion and resurrection of Jesus, leading to the core Christian goal of the remission of sin. Parallel stories aiming at the same goal: liberation of all people from enslavement, the remission of sin, and leading to at-one-ment with God. The psalmist reminds us, "He sent redemption to his people; he has commanded his covenant forever. Holy and awesome is his name" (Ps. 111:9). And Paul reminds every Christian, "In him we have redemption through his blood, the forgiveness of our trespasses, according to the riches of his grace" (Eph. 1:7).

Rev. Clark Williamson, a pioneer in Jewish-Christian dialogue in the early twentieth century, eloquently unpacks redemption in the Christian's life using images rooted in the Jewish Exodus, closing with a challenge to both Jews and Christians:

As we have been graciously freed from bondage to every earthly pharaoh, so we have become free for the task of setting others free from the bondages that enslave them. Faith is existence in this dual freedom. . . . The life of faith is both a liberated and a liberating life, both grace and ethics. Grace is the melody, ethics the lyrics, of Christian life . . . clearly, however real redemption is, it is far from complete. Slavery is not eradicated from the face of the earth, and therefore it is the mission of Israel and the Church to witness and work on behalf of God's liberating intent for all human beings.[81]

The Suffering Servant—Isaiah 53:4–11

Surely he has borne our infirmities and carried our diseases; yet we accounted him stricken, struck down by God, and afflicted. But he was wounded for our transgressions, crushed for our iniquities; upon him was the punishment that made us whole, and by his bruises we are healed . . . and the LORD has laid on him the iniquity of us all. He was oppressed, and he was afflicted, yet he did not open his mouth; like a lamb that is led to the slaughter. . . . By a perversion of justice he was taken away. Who could have imagined his future . . . although he had done no violence, and there was no deceit in his mouth. . . . The righteous one, my servant, shall make many righteous, and he shall bear their iniquities.

It comes as a surprise to many Jews and Christian that Isaiah 52:14–53:11 is literally an allegory about the Jewish people and the nation of Israel. This is clear if you read these passages in the previous chapters: 41:8–9, 42:1, 43:8, 44:1, 44:21, 45:4, 48:20, 49:3, and 49:6. In Matthew 12:15–18, its meaning is creatively extended to describe the Passion of Jesus. Jews throughout the centuries have used these verses as a kind of spiritual balm to explain their collective suffering. Do Jews have to suffer and "bear the iniquities" of the world? Did Jesus also have to die to fulfill this prophecy?

A powerful passage in the Younger Testament is based on Isaiah's suffering servant allegory: "He himself bore our sins in his body on the cross, so that, free from sins we might live for righteousness; by his wounds you have been healed" (1 Pet. 2:24). In Jewish terms of redemptive suffering, the Jewish people as a whole represent what Jesus stands for in Christianity. We might consider these passages in relation to the Crusades, the Inquisitions, the Holocaust—or any other act of genocide against any people—and understand how the persecution and suffering of any individual group can be used as an inspiration to do an act of *tikkum olam*, to make the world a better place.

John's Gospel says, "For God so loved the world that he gave his only Son, so that everyone who believes in him may not perish but may have eternal life" (John 3:16). From a Jewish perspective (or a universalist Christian one), this passage could be applied to all innocent people who suffer and could be interpreted to say: God so loved the world that he gave his only begotten sons and daughters—Isaac bound on the altar, the Hebrew slaves, Aaron's sons, Jesus, Akiva, the martyrs of Masada, Jews expelled from Spain, African American slaves, Native American victims of Manifest Destiny, victims of the Holocaust, victims of all genocides, Martin Luther King, and any innocent child or adult who suffers—so that everyone who expresses empathy for them "may not perish but may have eternal life."

One of Judaism's great twentieth-century spiritual masters, Rabbi Abraham Isaac Kook, wrote *The Lights of Penitence*, a classic on repentance. He outlines the Jewish conception of why righteous individuals suffer on behalf of humanity. In addition to those innocents mentioned above, Christians will surely be reminded of their beloved Jesus in Rabbi Kook's words about the suffering of innocent people:

> The few noble spirits who seek the light of God suffer because of the sins of society as a whole. Their love for people is boundless. The core of the good in their souls is drawn especially toward the good of society and society is prone to contaminate them with the sins in which it is enmeshed. However, the truly righteous suffer willingly all the obstructions, all the physical and spiritual suffering, their only concern is to service their goal, to enlighten, to improve, to enhance the good and the light of holiness, to hew a path toward the light of God and His delight, that it might enter every heart and spirit so that all may enjoy the goodness of the Holy One, that God might rejoice in His works.[82]

The suffering of others has a vicarious effect upon those who empathize and identify with that suffering. This is the key to unlocking the mystery of redemption and to a deeper understanding of both the Exodus and the Cross. If the suffering of others aligns us with and makes us a part of them, we are brought into the fold, into alignment with all of suffering humanity. A powerful Midrash offers us the unsettling notion that the Messiah accepts suffering not just willingly, but with a sense of gladness in the knowledge that the suffering is not meaningless; that it is done for the sake of others; that it will redeem them; and that it will bring them closer to God:

> The Messiah will say: "Master of the Universe, with joy in my soul and gladness in my heart I take this suffering upon myself, provided that not one person in Israel perish; that not only those who are alive be saved in my days, but that also those who are dead: who died from the days of Adam up to the time of redemption; and not only these be saved in my days, but all those who died as miscarriages; and that not only these be saved in my days, but all those whom You thought to create but were not created. Such are the things I desire, and for these I am ready to take upon myself."[83]

In Jewish theology, this salvation that the Messiah speaks about is not so much about the spiritual plane of the afterlife, as it is about physical rescue from harm and injustice. Redemption is less about the soul than it is about deliverance from worldly oppression and tyranny, as exemplified by the Exodus narratives. In a commentary on the work of C. S. Lewis, the great twentieth-century Christian writer and Princeton University professor Dr. Leora Batnitzky writes:

> Christianity is defined by affirming the role and necessity of suffering for human beings. The Son of God suffered unto the death, not that men might suffer, but that their suffering

might be like his. Lewis holds that Christianity is defined by affirming the role and necessity of suffering for human beings. Christ does not end suffering but is the model for it.[84]

And what does the model show? That suffering is not meaningless. Christians who empathize with Jesus's suffering are "saved" from their own isolation and alienation from God. When people have empathy for just one person's suffering, it connects them to all human suffering. It is our identification with one another's pain that brings meaning to our own lives—it's what makes us human.

In the Tanakh, the word *nasa*, meaning "suffer," is not used exclusively about feeling pain. Often, it implies that people bear or put up with something and has a neutral or even positive meaning. Hebrew words based on the *nasa* root mean to "bear a load" and also "to lift up," "to exalt." This is mirrored in English. When the King James translators had Jesus saying, "Suffer the little children to come unto me, and forbid them not" (Mk. 10:14), they were obviously meaning "allow." This meaning of suffering as "allowing" or "bearing" relates to C. S. Lewis's understanding of the Cross as a model for suffering.

How does this relate to the suffering of the Jewish people? Throughout history despotic rulers made Jews suffer just for practicing their faith. On Passover, Jews read a tragic prophecy in the Haggadah: "In every generation our enemies rise against us to destroy us but the Holy One, blessed be He, saves us from their hand." To the sages and rabbis, suffering was the consequence of standing up for the ideals and *mitzvot* of the Torah. Suffering is not glorified, romanticized, or idealized in Judaism; it is simply accepted as a reality. The innovation of Christianity was to ask its followers to participate in Jesus's suffering, and to hallow that suffering as expiation for past sins and as the means of liberation from future sins.

For Jews, the literal meaning of the passages in Isaiah 53 describe the Jewish people as a whole: "He [Israel] was wounded for our transgressions, crushed for our iniquities; upon him was the punishment that made us whole, and by his bruises we are healed" (Isa. 53:5). This passage is interpreted in the Talmud as applying to Moses as well:

> God said about Moses, "Because he poured out his soul to death, and was numbered with the transgressors; 'Yet he bore the sins of many because he secured atonement for the making of the Golden Calf. And made intercession for the transgressors' . . . because he begged for mercy on behalf of the sinners in Israel that they should turn in penitence."[85]

Moses was the redeemer for the children of Israel—his suffering and intercession resulted in God reaffirming the covenant with the Jewish people. Christianity followed in this interpretive tradition and applied the passage to Jesus. Yet Dr. Batnitzky highlights the subtle difference between the way Jews and Christians understand redemptive suffering:

> For many strands of the Christian tradition, this redemption involves participating in the suffering of Christ, the light and the redeemer of humankind. For the Jewish tradition, in contrast, the central historical and scriptural event is God's choice of and covenant with the people of Israel, a choice and covenant that remain unbroken.[86]

The key to understanding the redemptive aspect of suffering for Jews is the centrality of the notion of *britt,* "covenant," in Judaism. Jews have an unbreakable contract with God. Loyalty to that covenant has caused ongoing martyrdom of the Jewish people, who acknowledge—not always "willingly" or with "gladness"—the reality of their suffering until the Messiah comes. To the Jew there is no need to ennoble suffering through any special doctrine—it has already been ennobled through that covenant. After all, by Israel's "stripes" others are healed. As we've mentioned, the Exodus from Egypt was more than an intellectual model for African Americans; it was redemptive. It had real spiritual power—the story was not only a model for liberation but also for redemptive suffering. An energetic exchange is made whereby the suffering of the Jewish people, or any people, elicits empathy and compassion from others.

The rabbis teach that when the righteous suffer, God suffers too. This certainly seems to be part of the message of the Cross as well. "When a person suffers, what does the *Shekhinah* [the feminine Presence of God] say? 'My head is heavy, my arm is heavy.' If the Holy One, blessed be He, is thus grieved over the blood of the wicked, how much more so over the blood of the righteous that is shed" (Talmud: Hagigah 15b).

Rabbi Irving Greenberg asks, "Where was God during the Holocaust?" His answer:

God was with people ("I will be with him in distress" Ps. 91:15)—being tortured, degraded, humiliated, murdered. Where else would God be when God's loved ones were being hounded and destroyed? So, how were the rabbis able to justify the suffering of the innocent and the righteous? They recognized that there was retributive suffering in this world— that sometimes a person suffers for his/her misdeeds. But they also saw another kind of suffering whereby the innocent suffer for the sins of their community or the nation. Finally, there is the sense within Judaism that having a covenantal relationship with God does not make life easier, but actually even more challenging. God says: You alone have I singled out of all the families of the earth—this is why I will call you to account for all your iniquities (Deut. 3:2).[87]

It is always difficult to understand the suffering of the innocent, but the rabbis teach that not all suffering is punishment for sins as we see in the Suffering Servant passages in Isaiah 53. In the Midrashic writing called *Mekhilta de Rabbi Ishmael*, Rabbi Meir sees that the people of Israel weigh their good deeds against their suffering, and then wonder why

God allows them to suffer. The Holy One assures them: "The deeds that you have done and the suffering that I have brought upon you—not according to your deeds have I brought suffering upon you." Christians knows this well through the sacrificial suffering of their Messiah. And King Solomon confirms this principle: "For the LORD reproves the one he loves, as a father the son in whom he delights" (Prov. 3:12).

If Christ's suffering brings Christians to see the Cross in everyone's suffering, then Christians will do all they can to help relieve the suffering of others. If Israel's suffering brings Jews to see their suffering in everyone's suffering, they will do all they can to relieve the suffering of others. Without radical empathy, what is a Christian? What is a Jew? Without taking action to relieve suffering, there can be no Jew, there can be no Christian.

The great Catholic writer and mystic Thomas Merton warns us of the danger of confusing the innocent who suffer with divine punishment for sin. He startles the reader with his understanding of anti-Semitism, which he calls theological suicide:

> The theology of suffering is strongly tinged with ideas of punishment, and morality becomes a morality of obedience rather than love. In this aggressive, solemn, dark and feudal Christianity . . . there grows up the hatred and contempt of the Jew, whose role is more and more that of the theological Christ-killer on whom the curse has fallen. But perhaps there was in this a deep unconscious guilt for Christians who did not truly understand Christ.[88]

For Merton, to understand Christ is to comprehend the irony that Jesus seems to have failed when he is taken to the cross, but that it is out of failure that he becomes "a light unto the nations." Christians see themselves in Jesus precisely because he suffered as they do. This theology is deeply rooted in the redemptive suffering of the Jewish people. Some people empathize with the Jewish people; others want to destroy them. Jesus is a precise microcosm, a fractal if you will, of the nation in which he was born. People followed him, hoping he was the Messiah, and the Romans wanted to destroy him because he might have been the Messiah. Dr. Robert Gibbs of the University of Toronto is aware of how the Jewish people's courageous practice of self-criticism has historically been used against them. He writes:

> The Jewish texts subject our people to severe criticism and interpret our suffering as suffering for the sake of others, precisely by accentuating self-criticism and by holding out hope for redemption through suffering. But to use the others' suffering as proof of their sin and of their deserved punishment is to misread these texts. Such justification of Jewish suffering by Christians has made it almost impossible for Jews to continue to recognize any meaning in our own suffering.[89]

A final point in Professor Batnitzky's essay addresses the impact of Jewish suffering upon the world. She quotes one of the most influential Jewish philosophers of the nineteenth century, Hermann Cohen. I think that Christian readers will see their own Messiah in Cohen's words:

> Hermann Cohen (1842–1918) argued perhaps most explicitly that Judaism was defined in terms of its vicarious capacity to suffer for others. According to Cohen, this view is the proper interpretation of suffering servant: "As Israel suffers, according to the prophet, for the pagan worshippers, so Israel to this very day suffers vicariously for the faults and wrongs which still hinder the realization of monotheism."[90]

In the autumn of 2006, I was appalled by religious leaders from the three great monotheistic traditions as they pronounced with arrogant certainty "the reason" why God had allowed Hurricane Katrina to devastate Louisiana, Mississippi, and the Gulf Coast. Their profane interpretations did exactly what Thomas Merton warned about in confusing divine punishment for sin and the suffering of the innocent. A Christian minister said that Katrina was God's punishment for the sins that take place in New Orleans. A Muslim sheikh said it was Allah's punishment for America's support of Israel. An Israeli rabbi said that it was God's punishment for President Bush's support of the Israeli withdrawal from Gaza. How could they speak that way? They worship petty gods. Shame on anyone who thinks they can know the mind of God and can declare why others suffer.

Learning from Suffering

Was the enslavement of the Hebrews a prerequisite for the birth of the nation of Israel? Couldn't it have been done without such misery? Was the suffering of Jesus a prerequisite for the birth of Christianity? Weren't the teachings of the Gospels enough?

Here is a story of how suffering and rejection led to something good for one man in the generation just before Jesus—and it is possible that Jesus heard of this incident. Hillel and Shammai are two of Judaism's great first-century sages, yet they often had opposite opinions about theology and law (differences that continue in Judaism today). A Gentile seeker comes to Shammai and says, "I'll convert to Judaism if you can stand on one foot while telling me the meaning of the whole Torah." Shammai picks up a stick and threatens to hit the man. Shaken, the seeker goes to Hillel and makes the same challenge: "I'll convert to Judaism if you can stand on one foot while telling me the meaning of the whole Torah." Hillel lifts a foot off the ground and speaks: "What is hateful to you, do not do to your neighbor: that is the whole Torah. The rest is commentary. Now go and study." The man leaves, studies, and eventually converts to Judaism.

Rabbi Zalman Schachter-Shalomi liked to point out that it is the harshness of Shammai that opens the man's heart to be able to receive the Golden Rule of Hillel. What Hillel says in one sentence might not have been meaningful to the Gentile without having had a contrasting experience. It gave the man the very foundation he needed to understand what Hillel was saying. It was because of his suffering that his heart was open to receive the wisdom of Hillel.

Is the same principle true of how each of us gains insight? Do we need to be chased away by Shammai in order to comprehend the wisdom of Hillel? If the seeker had gone to Hillel first, would he have experienced such a powerful spiritual awakening? If Judaism had not begun in the agony of enslavement, would the beloved memory of the Patriarchs and Matriarchs been enough to lead the Hebrews into nationhood? It is unlikely. In the same manner, if Christianity had not begun in the agony of the Crucifixion, would the teachings of the Gospel have been enough to inspire the Gentile world to form a new religion? Again, it is unlikely.

This should not be taken to justify cruelty, but it does mean that we can learn from the terrible trials we all face. The Jewish people learned empathy from their experience as slaves. The American colonists learned of the importance of democracy because of oppression from the British. Like the Israelites of old, Black Americans in slavery learned the value of freedom from their suffering. Even now Native Americans, Jews, Armenians, Rwandans, Sudanese, Syrians, and others around the world grappling with issues of terrorism, mass murder, and genocide struggle to understand what good can be redeemed from such horror. It is not easy. As Hillel told the man, "Now go and study."

Appropriation or Misappropriation

PART FOUR
Appropriation or Misappropriation

If the Exodus were a piece of modern literature, there would be dozens of lawsuits over competing rights to the story. Jews would claim proprietary rights since the story is about their ancestors. Supersessionist Christians would claim rights of inheritance, arguing that Christ, as the Lamb of God, has replaced the Passover. Groups within Christianity would sue and countersue for damages resulting from heretical interpretations. African Americans would assert their position that 400 years of slavery entitled them to unrestricted usage of the story. Native Americans would charge abuse caused by application of the Bible's conquest narratives. Secular socialists would join the fracas to assert that the story has always been in the public domain and is not subject to copyright protection.

I know of no other epic saga that has been used in so many different cultural, political, and religious contexts. The liberation of the Hebrews occurred over 3,300 years ago, but as recently as the 1960s it was the centerpiece of a struggle of liberation: the civil rights movement in America. Rival groups have used and misused its components—one group espousing freedom, another conquest; one group supporting victims, another rationalizing invasion—each selecting only the components of the story that justify their cause.

The term *appropriation* generally describes the conscious acquisition and use of something without permission of the owner. In the context of the Exodus story, I am using the term in this way: *Appropriation* uses the story for the benefit of both the appropriator *and* the original community. *Misappropriation*—encompassing colonial blunders—uses tropes from the story for the benefit of only the appropriator and at times to the detriment of others.

The Complexity of the Question

Who determines if the use of a song, story, ritual, or ritual object from a particular spiritual tradition is appropriation or misappropriation? When my friend Father Mike Walker asked me what I thought of his church hosting a Catholic seder, I told him I was uncomfortable with the idea, but that a respectful alternative would be for him to invite a member of the Jewish community to lead a model seder for his community. I explained how missionary groups have misappropriated the seder in attempts to entice Jews into converting to Christianity, or otherwise "prove" that the Jewish Passover was merely a prefiguration of Jesus as the Lamb of God.

In judging the use of an element from another spiritual tradition, we must ask: "Will it be used for justice or dominance? Will it be used for coercion or encouragement? Is it merely decorative or authentic? Do I have permission from the leadership of the other tradition to use the element?" With these criteria, an example of positive appropriation is the use of the 1872 black spiritual "Go Down, Moses" in Jewish seders throughout the United States. While the song originated in African American slave culture its narrative is of the Jewish Exodus. When used cross-culturally, as long as there is no harm or gain by one group to another its use is appropriate. Furthermore, use of the Exodus motif as an important theme in the abolitionist and the civil rights movements is not just appropriate, but praiseworthy, as it contributes to the goal of liberation of an oppressed people.

The determination between cultural appropriation and misappropriation is nuanced. While the Exodus story has been used for justice and freedom to worship, it has also been used to repress the worship and freedom of others. Liberation theology used the Exodus story to help bring about social reforms in the 1960s and 1970s in Brazil, which benefitted people oppressed under military rule. This was a beneficial use of the story.

Conversely, this theology has been used to confirm anti-Semitic beliefs about Jews, Judaism, and Israel. In the seventeenth century, the Puritans appropriated the Exodus story in their struggle to reform the Church of England. However, they simultaneously used it in missionary work to justify persecution and violence against Native Americans. Theology professor Dr. Cheryl A. Kirk-Duggan wisely asks us to use "careful consideration" in the application of the Exodus story. She writes,

> Scholars and believers use Exodus to find hope, strength, and inspiration to resist and overcome. Exodus inspires some to confront and overthrow tyranny, others used it to generate and preserve tyranny; to justify oppression and domination. Themes of oppression and liberation are both evident, emerging from the nature and use of power in Exodus. Careful considerations of these topics is critical to keep Exodus from becoming a narrative of conquest.[91]

It's crucial to read the Exodus in its full biblical context. The books of Exodus, Numbers, and Deuteronomy detail the communal courage, insecurity, and fears of the Israelites during their forty-year trek. However, the wilderness journeys must be studied in the context of passages in the books of Joshua and Judges that outline the military battles in the settlement of Canaan. Though sometimes labeled the "conquest of Canaan," the term is not quite accurate and needs a bit of explanation. The liberated slaves saw themselves as returnees to the land of their ancestors, since the biblical patriarchs and matriarchs had lived in Canaan hundreds of years before, inhabiting it for four generations. The Hebrews and Canaanites were both ethnically Semitic, speaking similar languages, with overlapping cultures. Some scholars suggest that the settlement of Canaan was a combination of military conquest and natural assimilation—the Israelites assimilated into Canaanite culture, and the Canaanites came to accept the emerging Israelite theology of a single Deity.

Historical inquiry demands a thoughtful response. By our modern sensibilities, the violence involved in the settlement of Canaan by the newly freed Hebrew slaves is not equivalent to the Anglo-European military conquest of Native territories in America. The Europeans were not returning to the land of their ancestors as the Hebrews were. The battles described in the Bible to settle Canaan, though, are brutal and disturbing, but so are all wars. However common for that time, the violence should be neither minimized nor used to justify violence or terrorism today. It is interesting that these same battles that disturb our modern sensibilities were used as inspirational stories by African slaves in the struggle for emancipation in America. Dr. John Coffey tells us, "Joshua's storming of the Promised Land appealed to the weak at least as much as it did to the strong. It had an important place in the imagination of African Americans, including the leaders of slave revolts."[92]

There are four main parts to the Exodus saga: the enslavement of the Hebrews, the Passover liberation, the forty years of journeying in the Sinai Peninsula, and the settlement of Canaan. When a colonizing nation uses only the fourth part of the saga to justify its conquest by describing the people they conquer as Amalekites, Midianites, or Moabites, it is a disingenuous misappropriation of the Exodus.

Although the Hebrews did not justify the settlement of Canaan by ethnic or cultural differences, as was done with the conquest of the Americas, Dr. Scott Langston cautions us to acknowledge the contrary ways the Exodus has been used, and the ambiguous peculiarities of the biblical narrative itself:

> The Exodus has been influential in articulating the struggle against tyranny and has also been used to characterize the resistance of the tyrannical to struggles for freedom. At the same time, it has evoked reflection on the oftentimes violent measures used to gain freedom, as well as on the role of God in bringing about calamity. . . . The appeal of Exodus to oppressed and oppressor alike reflects the book's view of

the tenuous and precarious nature of power. Power is not one-sided or one-dimensional; nor is Exodus simply a book pitting good against evil. The thin line between good and evil becomes evident in the use of Exodus, and the power of its ideas makes it a potentially dangerous book. It can bring about great good, but it can also create great evil.[93]

More than ever, Jews, Christians, and Muslims need to celebrate the unique ways each religion has applied the Exodus story in the service of freedom. At the same time, we must all take special care to understand how Native American tribes ended up on the receiving end of the conquest narrative of the same story. The age of triumphalist readings and justification of violence from all Scriptures needs to come to an end.

For a Jew to fully understand the liberation of the slaves in the Exodus saga, and for Christians to understand liberation from sin by the death of Jesus, it would be wise for all the faithful in both traditions to study together and to turn to their common ancestor, biblical Judaism, for insight and answers.[94]

Exodus and the Christian Church

Christianity teaches that Jesus is the Paschal Lamb who "takes away the sin of the world" (John 1:29). *Paschal* is the Greek for Passover, and the paschal mystery and the image of Jesus as the Passover lamb is at the very heart of Christian theology. Regarding Christianity's relationship with Judaism, this appropriation has had both positive and negative consequences throughout the past two millennia. The Passover narrative is the first recorded story in history to celebrate the liberation of a slave population. It has been a powerful source of inspiration in the lives of Christians in their struggles for spiritual and communal freedom.

However, the early Church and most church fathers followed an interpretation called Replacement theology: the idea that Jesus as the Passover Lamb supersedes, completes, and replaces the Passover of the Jews. The Passover story is treated as a prefiguring or foreshadowing of its so-called fulfillment in the Christ story. With this approach, Christian typology is an attempt to prove that the stories of the "old" testament have been superseded by new and "better" ones. Dr. Langston states:

> The Christianizing of the exodus story thus contributed not only to Christian claims of superiority, but also to Christian hostility toward Jews and Judaism. Its continued growth is reflected in the Emperor Constantine's comments to those not attending the Council of Nicaea, that, "It was declared to be particularly unworthy for this, the holiest of all festivals (i.e., Easter), to follow the custom of the Jews (i.e., Passover), who had soiled their hands with the most fearful of crimes, and whose minds were blinded."[95]

Dr. Langston points out that Origen, an influential third-century church father, "expresses hostility toward Jews, especially when he equates them with the Egyptians, subtly implying that they should suffer a similar fate. He also associates the church with the departing Israelites, and Jews and Judaism with pharaoh and Egypt." He adds a sad historical fact that in the first few centuries of the Common Era, "Christians began using the exodus tradition not merely to draw distinctions between Judaism and Christianity, but to condemn Jews, even transmitting such contempt to the laity through the liturgy."[96]

We are reminded by Dr. Langston that another church father, Melito of Sardis, used the Exodus as a foil to condemn the Jews for the murder of Jesus as he "takes the central event in Judaism and uses it to condemn Jews and assert Christian superiority."[97] Replacement theology is found as early as the first century. For example, in the book of Acts, Barnabas says that Moses holding up his arms when battling Amalek is a prefiguration of Jesus on the cross. Many Younger Testament verses improperly translated, or read out of context, are prone to supersessionist interpretations.

We cannot dismiss tragic past events between Synagogue Jewish and Church Christian relations as ancient history. Just as racism is systemic in Anglo-European culture, so is an unconscious, and often unintentional, form of anti-Semitism systemic in traditional Christian theology. Replacement theology is alive and well in many churches, and this in turn gives rise to religiously justified anti-Semitism, passed down generation after generation. At the same time, it is important to acknowledge that since the Holocaust, many pastors and priests throughout the world have worked hard to understand the Passion narrative in such a way that the impression is not given that the Jews are "Christ killers." Many Christian theologians have worked hard to reinterpret Younger Testament verses that have been used to bolster Christian triumphalism and inadvertent anti-Semitism.

Will the Real Israel Please Stand?

Dr. John Coffey reviews the way the Protestant Reformation used the bondage and liberation of the children of Israel in breaking away from the Catholic Church. A 1524 publication called Martin Luther "a modern Moses leading the faithful out of Egyptian darkness towards the light of the crucified Christ."[98] The slogan "Christian liberty" was used in the Reformation, casting Luther as a liberator from the bondage of the popes. Dr. Coffey writes:

> If Exodus mattered to British Protestants in the 1550s, it was to become even more important to Dutch Calvinists as they fought to liberate their country from Spanish bondage. As historian Simon Schama points out, the Israelites' long trek to freedom "had a particularly literal relevance for a founding generation of Netherlanders, 150,000 of whom had physically left the fleshpots of the south, crossed formidable water barriers and reached a land of abundance."[99]

Calvinists, like the Pilgrims and Puritans, portrayed themselves as "new Israelites." Other groups, like the Quakers, Mormons, and many denominations in the African American church, did the same later in American history. From the first centuries of the Common Era, the idea of the church being the "new Israel" has been at the center of Christian theology. But if the church is new Israel, what is to be done with old Israel, the Jewish people who were scattered throughout Europe, North Africa, and the Middle East?

Christian sects and denominations have competed over who represents this so-called new Israel—who is spiritually redeemed and who will partake in the heavenly Promised Land. In the eighteenth century, tensions were high between the Puritans and Quakers, both sects vying for supremacy in their use of Exodus imagery.

The Puritans saw America as the new Canaan, while Quakers considered the restrictive Puritan rules to be a type of Egypt. In response, some Puritans like clergyman Samuel Fisher compared Quaker leadership to the "counsellors of Egypt." Within Christianity today, the struggle goes on between some denominations as to who is the authentic heir to the Israelite tradition, and who can authentically declare the Exodus story as exclusively theirs.

These in-house struggles within Christianity have caused ongoing danger and distress for the Jewish people since the second century. Why danger? Why distress? First, the Jews never relinquished their covenant, the one supposedly replaced. There is no heir to the Hebrew covenant except the modern Jewish people. Jews often see the use of the Exodus story by non-Jews as laudable (e.g., abolitionism, liberation from colonialism, and the civil rights movement). The problem arises when appropriation becomes misappropriation—when the Mosaic covenant is considered nullified; when a denomination declares itself to be the "new" Israel, and Jewish people are treated as the "new" Gentiles who need to accept Christ in order to be saved. Some Mormons actually call Jews "Gentiles," who, like all other "non-believers," need baptism.

Missions aiming to get Jews to convert to Christianity usually target the most vulnerable populations: the elderly, the poor, the frightened, and the assimilated Jews who know little of their heritage. Some of the arguments used to get these people to convert are a form of spiritual bribery. It's one thing to present the Gospels to a potential convert, but the missionaries promise eternal damnation without Christ. To the question "Will the real Israel please stand?" the answer is simple: they are already standing. They never sat down.

Exodus and the Puritans

In the sixteenth century, Puritans used the Exodus stories of the settlement of Canaan against Native Americans. Dr. Coffey points out that "because the focus was on possessing the Promised Land, some New Englanders were able to turn the biblical story against the native inhabitants. More than one writer who compared New England to Canaan also identified the local tribes as Canaanites or Amalekites."[100] One needs only to study the tragic Pequot War of 1636 to see the devastating effect of Puritan triumphalism against Native people in New England. Believing they were living in a new Canaan, Puritan religious leaders appointed missionaries who would coerce Native people to convert with the promise of eternal life rather than eternal hell because they were not Christian. The Puritans established fourteen "praying towns" in New England where Indians lived in Puritan-like settlements. They weren't permitted to use their own languages, clothing, customs, and sacred rituals.

In describing the Puritan Revolution, seventeenth-century preacher Dr. Thomas Goodwin declared: "the only parallel of God's dealing with us that I know in the world [is] . . . Israel's bringing out of Egypt through a wilderness, by many signs and wonders towards a place of rest."[101] He, along with British military leader Oliver Cromwell, thought of the Exodus in triumphalist terms against indigenous peoples. Coffey gives us a good example of how the Puritans used the Exodus story:

> Throughout the 1640s and 1650s, no story captured the imagination of the godly quite like this one. Exodus provided a way of reframing and making sense of England's troubles. The Parliamentarians were not seditious rebels; they were the oppressed children of Israel, suffering under Egyptian taskmasters, and then being led out of bondage by Mosaic leaders.[102]

It's ironic that what is called Hebraism was venerated in some of America's oldest and most respected universities such as Harvard, Dartmouth, and Yale that were started by Puritans. Unlike other Christian colleges, they taught the Hebrew language and studied the Hebraic roots of Christianity. In the eighteenth century, it was not hard to find beliefs among Puritan leaders, and later among Congregationalist pastors who lived in New England, that were friendly toward Judaism. Theology professor Dr. Wayne Rollins outlines the "striking irony" in the ways the Exodus has been employed:

> Ideological critics draw attention to a striking irony, namely that a biblical text may be liberating for one person or group but oppressive to another. . . . When refracted through the experience of liberationist theologians and civil rights leaders, the Exodus functions as a symbol of freedom. But refracted through the experience of the Native American, whose identity is not with the conquering Israelites but with the invaded Canaanites, it becomes a symbol of oppression. Robert Allen Warrior, an Osage Indian, contends that the Exodus saga provided Puritans and other European settlers in North America with a biblical text whose particular ideological reading justified the destruction of indigenous peoples.[103]

Exodus in Colonial American History

The eighteenth-century fight for freedom from England was one of the first modern attempts to uproot colonialism and replace it with democracy. The American Revolution, and the Constitution that came out of it, inspired the French and dozens of other liberation movements and struggles for majority rule over the past two and a half centuries. Its moral underpinnings were inspired by the Exodus. How ironic it is that some of America's most venerated founding fathers, like George Washington and Thomas Jefferson, owned slaves. In Jefferson, one can imagine a man haunted by his own duplicity. Or worse, maybe he wasn't haunted. (Benjamin Franklin was also a slave owner but later repented and became an abolitionist along with Alexander Hamilton.)

Irony is a word I cannot avoid repeating when it comes to the use of the Exodus story by Puritans and American revolutionaries. The story was used to advance their own causes for freedom, while they selectively ignored the moral commandments of the Bible when it came to Native Americans and African Americans. As Dr. Coffey acutely points out, "If American Puritans had crossed the ocean or fought the War of Independence to find a new Canaan, Africans had been forcibly ripped from their Promised Land and transported to a new Egypt."[104] From the other side of the pond, we have the irony of a British Empire that opposes independence for the colonies but has already abolished slavery.

Critical of the colonists fighting for freedom, English Anglican writer Samuel Johnson called out colonial hypocrisy in 1775 when he wryly asked, "How is that we hear the loudest yelps for liberty among the drivers of negroes?" Johnson was an opponent of slavery based on Christian moral principles. According to biographer James Boswell, he once proposed a toast to the "next rebellion of the negroes in the West Indies."*

---

* Johnson is also reputed to have described the French and the English as "two robbers stealing land from the indigenous people of North America."

It's ironic that more of the colonialists fighting for freedom from the British—some even described themselves as "a race of slaves" in servitude to England—did not oppose slavery and the barbarous policies against Native Americans. Taking a panoramic look at American history and its use of the Exodus, Rabbi Lance J. Sussman shines light on the shadowy side of the story's misappropriation:

> The biblical story of the Exodus also casts a moral shadow across darker episodes in American history. The "Trail of Tears" removal of Native people under President Jackson, the short-lived 1862 expulsion of American Jews by General Grant from areas under his command in the South, and the internment of Japanese-Americans during World War II all have qualities of being an anti-Exodus unworthy of either the biblical Exodus or the American promise of freedom. Increasingly problematic among American Jews was the American failure to lead a redemptive Exodus of Jews from Europe during the final years of the Holocaust.[105]

It should not be overlooked that Christian activism in the abolitionist movement helped topple the institution of slavery. Quakers, followed by Anglicans, Presbyterians, some Baptists, and evangelicals of many denominations were active in the opposition to slavery. Dr. John Coffey sums up the role of Christian denominations in the abolition of slavery:

> Only gradually, from the mid-eighteenth century onwards, did a Christian abolitionist movement take shape. It began with American Quakers around the 1730's. Slavery was also coming under attack from Enlightenment philosophers like Montesquieu and Rousseau, but it was Christian activists who initiated and organized an abolitionist movement.[106]

Exodus and African Americans

What an irony! Convert an enslaved African to Christianity, give her a Bible that features the book of Exodus—a manual for the liberation of people from slavery—and then expect her to be subservient. This did not go unnoticed by some slave owners who recognized that if the slaves read the Bible, with its demand for justice, they too might demand it. Yet it was impossible to restrain the missionaries. Most slave owners were "clever" enough to permit their slaves to be baptized but forbid them from reading—in part, to keep them away from the book of Exodus. But by the nineteenth century, there were too many emancipated slaves in both the South and the North who were literate and passionate about using the Exodus as a guide for ending slavery in America.

With the stories of Moses, Pharaoh, and Egypt, abolitionists had the perfect vehicle for creating a movement. And not just a vehicle, but certification from the Almighty that slavery was evil and that the schemes of the American pharaohs would fail. Even after the Civil War when things were going poorly under the oppressive Jim Crow laws, the black church had the stories of the Red Sea, Mount Sinai, and the crossing of the Jordan into the Promised Land to give them hope. Dr. Kirk-Duggan brilliantly summarizes the important work of African American studies scholar Dr. Eddie Glaude Jr. on the central place the Exodus held in the entire African American experience. She writes:

> African Americans use the term Exodus as religious, political, and socio-religious metaphor to make sense of middle passage, enslavement, and struggles for emancipation in the nineteenth century through liturgical drama of praying, preaching, and singing, disintegrating the space between enslaved peoples in ancient Egypt and colonial United States. . . . Using Exodus language of Egypt, covenant, wilderness, and Promised Land

was the political language of African American public life to unveil the suffering, violence, death, and hope that signified much African American reality. Used politically, Exodus language affords a critique that presses society to live up to its founding principles and ideals, embracing a God of justice and order, whose deliverance promises and grace meant the nation should also do justice in law and deed.[107]

In 1963 Rabbi Abraham Joshua Heschel startled an interfaith conference on interracial justice by challenging his audience with these words:

> At the first conference of religion and race, the main participants were Pharaoh and Moses. Moses' words were: 'Thus says the Lord, the God of Israel, let my people go that they may celebrate a feast to me.' While Pharaoh retorted: 'Who is the Lord, that I should heed this voice and let Israel go? I do not know the Lord, and moreover I will not let Israel go.' The outcome of that summit meeting has not come to an end. Pharaoh is not ready to capitulate. The exodus began, but is far from having been completed. In fact, it was easier for the children of Israel to cross the Red Sea than for a Negro to cross certain university campuses.[108]

One of the Reverend Martin Luther King's best friends and cofounder of the Southern Christian Leadership Council, Ralph Abernathy also invoked Moses and the Exodus in his talks. Referring to black soldiers who have given their lives for America in every war, he said: "Their bones are bleaching this very evening in every national cemetery and from their graves their silent cry to the pharaohs of injustice, inequality, segregation, discrimination and bigotry is, 'let my people go.'"[109] In 1965 Abernathy gave a talk where he referred to Moses's taking the emancipated slaves right to the border of the Promised Land before he died. It was an ominous forecast about the difficult road ahead, even though the Civil Rights Act had been passed. He said:

> When Moses walked into the courts of Pharaoh and thundered forth the call to "Let my people go," he introduced into history the concept of a God who was concerned about the freedom and dignity of all his children and who was willing to turn heaven and earth that freedom might be a reality. . . . It is this strong biblical tradition which has been the foundation of the freedom struggle for the past three centuries. As far back as the early days of slavery, black men heard the story of Moses and learned of this great God who would lead his people to freedom, and so they sang, "Go Down Moses." . . . And now we have come to the threshold of the Promised Land. We have shattered the legal barriers of segregation and discrimination, but there are new giants which await us in the land.[110]

The Hebrews may have left Egypt, but Egypt did not leave the Hebrews so easily. Unless a person has been a member of a persecuted minority, it is difficult to appreciate the generational trauma that affects the children's children of those who were victimized. The psychological scars can be seen in any culture that has suffered persecution. We see this in descendants of survivors of the Holocaust and other genocides, in the African American and Native communities, and in various Christian and Muslim minorities who have suffered persecution.

The misappropriation of the Exodus led to many negative consequences for the Jews of Europe, Native Americans, and African American Christians. The problem has not only been the misuse of story by oppressive regimes but, rather, the use of the story to create a systematized matrix of abuses and punishments for its victims. The logic of oppressive behavior goes like this: since the Jewish Passover has been replaced by the death of Jesus, then Jews are subject to the fate of all other heathens. If Native Americans are heathens, then Puritans or colonists can mistreat them with impunity. If a slave is less than human then biblical mandates of ethical treatment and human rights do not apply to them.

Anyone who has suffered under the self-righteous hatred of an oppressor can appreciate the righteous indignation of Frederick Douglass. This speech was delivered on July 5, 1852, a decade before the Emancipation Proclamation, and continues to provoke the conscience of people today. It was entitled *What to the Slave Is the Fourth of July?*

> It is the birthday of your National Independence, and of your political freedom. This, to you, is what the Passover was to the emancipated people of God. It carries your minds back to the day, and to the act of your great deliverance; and to the signs, and to the wonders, associated with that act, and that day. I am not included within the pale of this glorious anniversary! This Fourth of July is yours, not mine. You may rejoice, I must mourn. To drag a man in fetters into the grand illuminated temple of liberty, and call upon him to join you in joyous anthems, were inhuman mockery and sacrilegious irony. Do you mean, citizens, to mock me, by asking me to speak today? What, to the American slave, is your 4th of July? To him, your celebration is a sham . . . your shouts of liberty and equality, hollow mockery . . . There is not a nation on the earth guilty of practices more shocking and bloody than are the people of the United States, at this very hour.[111]

From Moses to Martin

Engraved on the tombstone of twelfth-century sage Moses Maimonides are these words: "From Moses to Moses there were none like Moses." Comparing someone to the biblical Moses is a rarely bestowed honor in Judaism, Christianity, or Islam. However, speaking of the nineteenth-century abolitionist Harriet Tubman, actor and writer Margaret Barton Driggs said, "To her own people she was, simply, 'Moses,' and their haunting spirituals—veiled messages—enlarged the metaphor to sing of Jordan and the Promised Land."[112] After the age of Maimonides there have been other courageous figures that have been worthy of being called Moses: Abraham Lincoln, Theodor Herzl, and Martin Luther King.

One cannot overstate the systemic racism that continues to infect most cultures around the world. Like a plague, until the medicine of civil rights legislation is mandated, the disease continues to be spread and passed down from generation to generation. This is what abolitionists like Frederick Douglass and Harriet Tubman faced in the nineteenth century, and it gives context to the fear many Americans had in response to the ministry of Martin Luther King. Within the civil rights community in the 1950s and 1960s there was a clear and steady trajectory toward anointing Rev. Martin Luther King a new Moses. The struggle to get the Civil Rights Act passed had been costly, and Exodus was the central theme for this new Moses, for black churches, and for the civil rights movement.

Rev. King did not appoint himself Moses, but he knew what people and the media were saying about him. His anointing came from the people. Like the biblical Moses who was reluctant to heed the call at the burning bush, King must have had doubts about accepting the role of a latter-day Moses. But he did accept the anointing, and he did it with humility. Listen to any of his speeches and you hear the voice of Moses and echoes of the Exodus. His prophetic sermon called "I See the Promised Land" was delivered on April 3, 1968, at the Bishop Charles Mason Temple in Memphis just hours before his assassination the next day:

> I don't know what will happen now. We've got some difficult days ahead. But it doesn't matter with me now. Because I've been to the mountaintop. And I don't mind. Like anybody,

I would like to live a long life. Longevity has its place. But I'm not concerned about that now. I just want to do God's will, and he's allowed me to go up to the mountain. And I've looked over. And I've seen the promised land. I may not get there with you. But I want you to know tonight, that we, as a people, will get to the promised land.[113]

Communications professor Dr. Gary Selby points out that the story of the Exodus gave the civil rights activists a sense of legitimacy. It gave them an explanation for both their successes and failures, and it authenticated their sense that Rev. King really was a Moses. The liberation of the Jews told the protesters there was a good end to their story—that justice would prevail, and they would enter the Promised Land. Dr. Selby writes:

The Exodus was a persistent theme in King's rhetoric throughout his career as spokesperson for the civil rights movement. Blacks were the chosen people of God, languishing in the Egypt of racial oppression. Significant events marking progress toward justice . . . were represented as the crossing of the Red Sea. The difficulties that blacks faced in pursuing racial equality were the travails of the wilderness, and the vision toward which they labored was the Promised Land of integration and brotherhood.[114]

Moses knew that the Israelites could never be truly free from oppression until the Egyptians were liberated from being oppressive. Rev. King, like Moses before him, knew that African Americans could never be free from the oppressive effects of racism until the oppressor Anglo-Americans were also free from their racism. Moses worked for the redemption of Egypt from its oppressiveness just as King worked for the redemption of white America from its racism. On many occasions King let his listeners know that he was also praying for white America, that they too needed to be liberated. The racism that Rev. King faced was rooted in ancient distortions of the story of Noah's son Ham as somehow being black and cursed. Dr. Coffey, however, points out:

> [T]he racist reading only emerged with the rise of the African slave trade, pioneered by Muslim Arabs and then taken up by Christian Europeans. Both groups needed to legitimize the dubious practice of enslaving black Africans, and they did so by claiming that their victims were descendants of Ham and so subject to Noah's curse. . . . A vulnerable text had become a text of terror.[115]

Many scholars have noted that the Exodus was the first recorded story in history of a slave population struggling for, and achieving, freedom. The ten plagues led to freedom, but the Hebrews had to face forty years of trials living in the wilderness. It was not a straight line from slavery to emancipation, or from emancipation to the Promised Land. As I've mentioned before, it was—like all growth and development—two steps forward and one step back at best. To the civil rights workers, sometimes it seemed like one step forward and two steps back. King, however, had a way of making the unsentimental realism of the Exodus narrative relevant to his supporters. He consistently drew upon the spiritual power of the experiences of the Hebrews to keep the civil rights movement's "eyes on the prize."

King applied the symbolism of the Exodus story in a simple and direct manner. For example, the Promised Land was associated with hope; crossing the Red Sea was associated with uncertainty; the story of the spies with setbacks; and conflicts within the civil rights movement with the ongoing complaining and squabbles among the Israelites.

In one particularly challenging moment, when the question was whether the government would enforce the Brown v. Board of Education decision, 25,000 people gathered for a Prayer Pilgrimage for Freedom rally. King stood at the Lincoln Memorial on May 17, 1957, and gave a message of hope while in the wilderness:

> Stand up for justice. (*Yes*) Sometimes it gets hard, but it is always difficult to get out of Egypt, for the Red Sea always stands before you with discouraging dimensions. (*Yes*) And even after you've crossed the Red Sea, you have to move through a wilderness with prodigious hilltops of evil (*Yes*) and gigantic mountains of opposition. (*Yes*) But I say to you this afternoon: Keep moving. (*Go on ahead*) Let nothing slow you up. (*Go on ahead*) Move on with dignity and honor and respectability. (*Yes*).[116]

In Liberation Theology

Liberation from oppression is a central theme in Torah, and Jesus too came to "release the oppressed." At first glance the idea of a theology based on liberation is in keeping with the values of the ethical commandments of the Torah and the Gospels of the Younger Testament: social justice, equality, taking care of those in need, land reform, and liberation from oppressors. Liberation theology tends to focus on structural, or corporate, injustices rather than on individual sin. At its best it seeks justice for the poor by protesting institutional injustice. Since its inception in the 1950s in Latin America, this theology has done some good in defense of the poor against brutal dictatorships, and in elevating the Gospel message of Jesus to apply to social justice issues.

Liberation theology developed within the Catholic Church, and has since spawned offshoots in black, Asian, and Palestinian religious communities. Proponents of liberation theology have taken stands on behalf of the poor in their struggles against corrupt religious and governmental institutions. The problem comes when this theology puts supersessionism into a strange brew of Marxist, anti-capitalist, and anti-Zionist dogmas. A modern anti-Semitism has emerged that does not necessarily focus on Jews or Judaism, but rather uses anti-Zionism and hatred for Israel as a cover for expressing prejudice. It is this kind of prejudice that plagues the writings of some of the theologians of liberation. Dr. Amy-Jill Levine summarizes the problem:

> In liberation theology—that form of religious thought proclaiming that God has a "preferential option for the poor" and seeking to put biblical pronouncement in service to political and economic ends—Jesus is the pedagogue of the oppressed, the redeemer of the underclass, the hero of the masses. The problem is not the use of Jesus for political ends;

the biblical material has always been (and should continue to be) used to promote a more just society. The problem is that the language of liberation all too often veers off into anti-Jewish rants. Jesus becomes the Palestinian martyr crucified once again by the Jews; he is the one killed by the "patriarchal god of Judaism"; he breaks down the barriers "Judaism" erects between Jew and Gentile, rich and poor, male and female, slave and free and so can liberate all today.[117]

The Palestinian Christian offshoot of liberation theology has the aim of all other supersessionist ideologies that preceded it, but with a unique twist. Instead of advocating the eradication of Judaism or the Jewish people using theological arguments, they challenge the existence of the nation of Israel. They try to avoid being labeled as anti-Semitic by claiming they aren't against Jews or Judaism, just Zionism and Israel.

The application of liberation theology against Israel is a prime example of misappropriation and egregious abuse of the biblical text and the Exodus story. Using the formation of the original Jewish state by the Hebrews after emancipation against the existence of the modern Jewish state, this group of Palestinian Christians claim to be the "true" or "new" Israel. This is nothing but replacement theology masquerading as social justice.

In attempting to bring "good news to the poor," liberation theology strays from its own good intentions when it divorces politics from the moral and spiritual obligations of both the Elder and Younger Testaments. As Mark Galli put it, "liberation theology as it usually comes to us seems more indebted to Marx than to Moses."[118] Too often this theology has been used to justify brutality under Marxist regimes (e.g., Cuba, Nicaragua, Venezuela, etc.), even while bravely struggling against secular or fascistic dictatorships.

Former Interfaith Affairs Director for the Anti-Defamation League, the late Rabbi Leon Klenicki, summed it up well:

Judaism certainly recognizes the Exodus as liberation, but maintains that the liberation from Egyptian bondage became meaningful only once Israel received the Law at Mt. Sinai. . . . These points are overlooked by . . . the theologians of liberation. They consider liberation as an end in itself not realizing that physical or economic oppression can only be overcome by freedom that has transcendental meaning. Otherwise, the liberation process ends in another form of tyranny or authoritarian dictatorship.[119]

In Every Generation:
Reappropriation within Judaism

Each year at Passover seders, Jews read two instructions in the Haggadah with the same thought-provoking phrase: *in every generation*. First it says, "In every generation there are those who seek to annihilate us, but the Holy One, blessed be He, saves us from their hands." Later in the seder the text says, "In every generation you ought to regard yourself as though you personally came out of Egypt. . . . The Holy One redeemed not only our ancestors, but also ourselves with them." Following the pattern of exile and redemption, Jews are reminded that in every generation they will face anti-Semitism and resistance to the covenant they received at Sinai. Yet, they are also reminded that they will be liberated by God, and that the story of the Exodus is to be understood as something beyond a single moment in time. Rabbi Greenberg sums up this sense of anamnesis within Judaism that is parallel to Christian thinking:

> The Exodus teaches us that history is not an eternal recurrence—ever repeating but never progressing—but a time stream with direction. History is not a meaningless cycle but the path along which the Divine-human partnership is operating to perfect the world. Time is linear, not merely circular; all humans are walking toward the end time when the final peace and dignity for humankind will be accomplished.[120]

The Exodus is an ongoing event, and the Jewish people in each generation are responsible for reappropriating and reinterpreting the story, in every culture where they live. Dr. Richard Sarason notes: "Jewish tradition itself is an ongoing act of religious/cultural re-appropriation and interpretation: in the constant juxtaposition between inherited past and experienced present, the two are mutually interpreting and interpenetrating."[121]

In the centuries before 1948, Jews generally retold the Passover story in relation to anti-Semitism, the suppression of their civil rights, and outright violence that was the experience of European Jewry. During the first half of the twentieth century, Zionists appropriated the Exodus theme in their struggle against the Ottoman and British occupation of the Holy Land.

Following the Holocaust, the British cruelly limited Jewish immigration into the Palestinian Mandate—a large swath of land that extended from the Mediterranean Sea to present-day Iraq. After World War I, the French and British colonists had been faced with dozens of national independence movements throughout the Middle East and Africa, including the Zionist Movement that sometimes defined itself as a fulfillment of the Exodus story. Zionism represented the right of the Jewish people to some part of their ancient homeland, not unlike the aspiration of the Israelites to return to their homeland in Canaan. The Palestinian Mandate was intended to have two states, one for the Arab population and one for the Jews.

After World War II, a boat appropriately named "Exodus 1947" carried more than 4,500 immigrants from the infernos of Europe to the shores of the British-controlled Palestinian Mandate. The British Navy rammed and seized the boat. The desperate immigrants were forced onto other deportation boats and sent back, as unbelievable as it sounds, to Germany. The outpouring of sympathy by the public was strong and the British altered their immigration policy, thereafter sending Jews fleeing Europe to detention camps in Cyprus, but not to what was to become an independent Israel.

One inspiring example of the Jewish appropriation of the Exodus occurred in the 1960s and 1970s when in the Soviet Union there was internal repression of Jews and severely restricted emigration to Israel. This inspired the formation of an international human rights crusade.

Throughout the campaign, the Exodus was the most prominent theme in the cause of freedom for Soviet Jewry.

In recent decades, hundreds of versions of the Haggadah have been published, or custom-made for individual families, to support various civil rights struggles. One of the first was called the "Freedom Seder," created by Rabbi Arthur Waskow a year after the assassination of Martin Luther King Jr.[122] Since then there have been Jewish seders dedicated to ending modern slavery, ending world hunger, ending terrorism against Israelis, and on behalf of feminism, LGBT rights, global justice, refugee rights, Tibetan freedom, peace, environmentalism, and many other causes. The Hagaddah has become the most popular vehicle for the creative retelling and application of the Exodus story by the Jewish people in the modern era.

Exodus Rivals—
Conclusion and Summary

The debate over appropriate use of the Exodus story has been going on since the beginning of Christianity, continuing through the Colonial Era, and into the present. In early American history, white Christians identified with the story as pilgrims leaving the Egypt of England to settle in a "new Israel," and many even called themselves Israelites. Black Christians, on the other hand, tended to identify with an earlier part of the story—they were Hebrews struggling with Moses for freedom. Two groups, each wanting freedom, using the same story to bolster their agendas. Dr. Scott Langston gives us a good summary of the main groups vying for authentic appropriation of the Exodus story:

> Enslaved African Americans understood themselves as God's people struggling against the pharaoh of American slaveholders, and abolitionists used it to denounce the institution of slavery. White southerners, however, considered themselves as contending against the pharaoh of the North who was intent on denying them their liberty by taking their property and independence. . . . Southerners invoked a tradition that Americans had employed in their struggle against the British pharaoh, George III. White Americans of the Revolutionary era had used the exodus to call for freedom from Great Britain, but with little thought of its application to African Americans, despite the latter's concurrent appeal to it.[123]

The rivalry gets even more convoluted. Dr. Coffey lists the various groups that depended on the Exodus to justify their own cause and negate the righteous causes of others: " . . . Catholics and Protestants, Parliamentarians and Royalists, Hanoverians and Jacobites, revolutionaries and abolitionists, blacks and whites, Democrats and Republicans."[124] All these groups ignored the plight of the real Hebrews, the Jewish people in their midst, and many Christians were slow to respond to the anti-Semitism that took root in the Promised Land of America. However, along with slavery, the greatest misuse of the Exodus was the land theft, massacre, and mass expulsions of Native populations from their own lands.

It's worth repeating that we must carefully consider how we use a sacred story from another religion. The biblical saga of the Exodus has been both righteously used and terribly misused over thousands of years, continuing to this very day. The moral imperative of the Exodus is the promulgation of freedom and justice—not the conquering of an oppressive enemy, but making the enemy into a friend.

PART FIVE
Personal Stories

The Answer Is Always the Exodus

My colleague Rabbi Shelley Waldenberg often explains the central role of the Exodus story in Jewish history with this reminiscence: "I believe in miracles, and I will tell you why," he will begin. You see, whenever his fifth-grade teacher of Tanakh, Mr. Markov, began talking, Shelley would become so bored he'd zone out and withdraw into his fantasy world where he played shortstop for the New York Yankees. One morning, his reverie was shattered: "Waldenberg! I asked you a question!" Mr. Markov shouted. "What did I ask?" Shelley froze. "One more time, Waldenberg, and you will be suspended!" After class that day, instead of going home, Waldenberg ran to his grandfather's house. The moment he walked in, his grandfather asked, "Shelley, what's wrong?" "Grandpa, I'm in trouble, big trouble, in my Tanakh class. Mr. Markov said if I don't pay attention he'll suspend me; and if he does, I know my dad will ground me for weeks. No baseball!"

His grandfather smiled, took a piece of paper, and wrote on it in Hebrew: "*Yetziat Mitzrayim,*" which means the Exodus from Egypt— words familiar to every Jew for the past 3,300 years, appearing in nearly every prayer, holiday, and festival. Once we were slaves in Egypt, and then God freed us so that we could go to Mount Sinai to receive the Ten Commandments. This is the centerpiece belief of Jewish civilization.

"So Shelley," his grandfather said, "if Mr. Markov calls on you, and you don't know the answer just say '*Yetziat Mitzrayim*' and you'll be fine." So Shelley went back to class and sure enough, Mr. Markov called on him when he wasn't listening. "All right, Waldenberg. Out! You will be suspended!"

When Shelley reached the door, he turned back to Mr. Markov, and muttered, "*Yetziat Mitzrayim.*" Mr. Markov appeared stunned. "Ha, ha Waldenberg! You are finally listening. *Mazal tov*! And you understand. More than understand. That was brilliant! It was not the answer I expected. But you saw a connection even I could not see!"

"So you see," Rabbi Waldenberg says today, "miracles do happen."

A Good Friday Miracle

In 2011, I was the interim rabbi for a small Jewish community in Portland, Oregon, called P'nai Or. Each month I traveled to Portland to lead services, teach Torah, and counsel members of the community. Services were held at St. Mark Presbyterian Church, where the large gold cross that hung in the front of the sanctuary was discretely covered with a piece of Jewish fabric art every Friday and Saturday for Shabbat services. St. Mark's spiritual leader, Rev. Barbara Campbell, quickly became my friend and colleague.

On a Wednesday evening in April of my third year at P'nai Or, Pastor Barbara called me in Ashland and said, "We have a problem."

"What kind of problem?" I was curious, since we always got along so harmoniously.

"A scheduling problem."

Even though the Jewish community schedules the sanctuary many months in advance, no one in either community had noticed that this particular Friday was also Good Friday, and they had double-booked the sanctuary.

There was a moment of silence while we pondered how to solve this, then Rev. Barbara drew in her breath, and said, "Let's celebrate Good Friday and Shabbat services together!" I could almost see her smiling through the phone.

"Oy Vey!" was the only response that echoed through my head, but I swallowed hard. "Um, Barbara, that might be difficult."

"Difficult?"

I explained to her that Good Friday is the one service that would be impossible for us do as an interfaith event. After all, Good Friday tells of the Passion and crucifixion of Jesus, usually told from the Gospel of John, which portrays the Jewish people in a horrible light, blaming them for the crucifixion. No Jewish congregation would feel comfortable, or even safe, joining that service.

"I see your point," she said.

We agreed to both pray about what to do and meet the next day when I arrived in Portland. Later Reverend Barbara told me: "From the moment I discovered the scheduling conflict, I felt a strange feeling that the Spirit was moving us toward something remarkable."

But when I walked into her office that Thursday afternoon, I wasn't feeling the Spirit, or sensing movement toward anything "remarkable." I felt only trepidation, more like I was walking into a fire. Barbara, however, was sitting up straight with the New Testament open on her computer. She was ready to roll.

"Let's rewrite some of the troubling verses" she said, drumming her fingers on the desktop.

"Um, you could do that?" I asked, looking at her dubiously.

"Of course," she said, "Christians have been doing that since the stories were first written down."

"Well, okay." I sat down across from her. This was going to be interesting.

"Is one of the problems that Judas's very name is related to the word 'Jewish'?" she asked.

I squirmed a little in my seat, just thinking about that painful association. "Well, er, yes, that is definitely a problem."

Barbara scrunched her eyebrows, "How about if we replace 'Judas' with 'The betrayer'?"

I nodded, trying not to gape as she did a search and replace.

"Better?" Barbara's jaw was set, her eyes bright.

I nodded dumbly. "Yes, better."

Barbara leaned back, pleased. Nothing could stop her now. "What about the Jews who hand Jesus over to Pilate? How about we replace that with 'A small band of corrupted leaders already in cahoots with the Romans handed Jesus over'? Is that better?"

I was beginning to like this. "Well, yes, actually, that would be excellent. Good call."

With what seemed like a holy, mad exuberance, she continued line by line, word by word, subbing phrases like "a puppet of Rome" for the "High Priest Caiaphas." "The Jews" was changed to "some of the leaders who were corrupt." Suddenly, she turned to me and stared.

"Rabbi David," she declared, "this is *so* courageous of you."

I gulped. "Courageous of me? You're the one rewriting your Holy Scriptures! I'm not courageous. We've been waiting two thousand years to change these words; it's you who are courageous!" We laughed and I felt some of my tension melt.

"All right," she continued, "if you're okay with doing the service together, you could start by lighting the Shabbat candles." Her face glowed, envisioning all the Christians and Jews in the shared light.

"We do a Tenebrae worship where we have seven candles, and we extinguish them one by one during the service until only the Christ candle remains." She gestured to show me how they snuffed each candle. With a final flourish, she said, "We'd extinguish the Shabbat candles last. Sound good?"

I took a deep breath and smiled weakly. "Um, well, no, um, not good. Barbara, we don't extinguish Shabbat candles. Ever."

"Oh, that's even better." She grinned at me. "We'll do it so the Shabbat candles are the only ones left burning: The light of Shabbat and the Jewish people can never be extinguished. I love it!"

My head was reeling. "One last thing," I said. "I so appreciate what you are trying to do, but I have to ask our community for their blessing. This is not a decision I can make alone."

I sent an e-mail out to the Jewish community explaining how Rev. Barbara and I had changed things and inviting them to this experimental, new service. I also suggested holding a regular Shabbat service in the social hall for those who were hesitant, while the rest of us were in the sanctuary with our Christian friends. The leadership agreed to move forward with this unique event.

On Friday evening, Reverend Barbara and I quietly prayed together at the door of the sanctuary before we walked side by side into the room.

I lit the two small Shabbat candles and chanted the blessing over the light. We spoke a few words of welcome, explaining about the need for changes to the traditional text. I told them Jesus had died as tens of thousands of Jews had died on crosses lining the streets outside Jerusalem in those terrible years. We read lines from Psalm 103 responsively as our Call to Worship:

"Bless the LORD, *O my soul, and all that is within me, bless his holy name."*

We then moved into a celebration of the Lord's Supper. As the ritual began I instinctively covered my head with my *tallit*, prayer shawl, and quietly murmured the Priestly Benediction that God instructed Aaron to bless people with more than 3,300 years ago. I raised up my arms and turned my hands toward the congregation as I began to whisper in Hebrew:

"May the Holy One bless you and protect you. May the Holy One shine His countenance upon you and be gracious to you. May the Holy One turn His countenance toward you and give you peace."

I realized I was a bit close to Rev. Barbara and her congregants, and wanted to offer them sacred space as they filed up to partake of the bread and wine representing the body and blood of Jesus. So I slowly moved backward, while the seven candles and Shabbat candles on the altar bathed the room in a quiet glow. I chanted Aaron's ancient prayer over and over as a mantra of gratitude for being able to participate in this long-awaited peace between Jews and Christians. I noticed that my arms were getting tired so I spread them out wider, farther and farther apart like the wings of an eagle. What I didn't realize was that as I backed up, toward the rear of the sanctuary, I'd planted myself directly in front of the large gold cross.

There I stood, a 63-year-old rabbi, my prayer shawl covering my head, with my arms spread wide in front of a cross. I was so caught up in my prayer trance that I hardly noticed the Christians participating in the service were gazing up at me, open-mouthed. One of them told me later that the shadows from the candles gave an eerie glow to my outline, but I had no idea what an image I was creating. A Jewish congregant told me later, "I was so shocked to see you like that. You looked like Jesus would have looked like if he had lived that long."

When the Communion section of the service was over, various church members slowly read the story of Jesus's Passion using the revised text from the Younger Testament that Pastor Barbara had created. Between the readings were familiar Good Friday hymns and dramatic scenes where contemporary characters speak about Tenebrae. Right after each Scripture reading, one of the seven candles was extinguished along with a row of lights in the room. In the end, only the Shabbat candles and the Christ candle remained lit in the pitch-black sanctuary. A few weeks later Pastor Barbara wrote this report about what happened later in the evening:

> As I carried the Christ candle slowly down the aisle and out of the sanctuary, one of our congregants later told me that the sorrow of Christians over the loss of Jesus and the quietness of Jews waiting each week by the light of two small Shabbat candles for their Messiah to come entwined in a very powerful way.
>
> It is easy to understand why many Jews today have never read this story. Though Rabbi David thanked St. Mark over and over for taking such a great risk, I could tell that it was an even greater risk for our Jewish friends to sit with us that night. . . . From the darkness of the sanctuary, silent worshippers slowly walked out into the night. A few shared tears and embraces. St. Markers went out into the darkness of the night to their homes. Our Jewish friends silently moved into the darkened fellowship hall nearby, not saying a word.
>
> Our time together was not about some sort of hope in the eventual merging of the Jewish and Christian faiths. Our time together was about knowing and honoring, with deep compassion, our respective redemption stories, and

regaining from each other vital aspects of faith that we had overlooked or
lost. The Spirit brought us together, has led us into times of study to open our
eyes, and has now brought us to worship together, celebrating a gracious,
redemptive God who continues to work miracles in our midst.

The Jewish community of P'nai Or was profoundly moved by this experience. As the Passion story was reenacted that evening with new language, my own heart opened to the suffering of Jesus along with tens of thousands of Jews in his era crucified and killed by the Romans. At the end of the story I was weeping. I had never cried for Jesus before. I didn't mourn for him as my messiah the way a Christian might, but as a rebbe, as a teacher, and fellow Jew. I silently recited the Kaddish, the Aramaic prayer for the dead that Jews chant to this day. It was the first time I had ever recited Kaddish for Jesus—I was reciting it for the Jewish Jesus who was called up for honors at the Torah as *Yehoshua ben Yosef v'Miriam*, Joshua son of Joseph and Miriam. These were new tears.

One St. Mark congregant later told Pastor Barbara it was the most meaningful worship of his entire life. *Dayanu*, as we sing in Hebrew each Passover, *dayanu*—that alone would have been sufficient. But there is so much more. The Good Friday ritual of the Jewish community coming together with the Christian community at St. Mark has continued every year since that first magical service that we created and experienced together.

The Seder As a Template

On Friday, December 30, 1994, I drove to Canterbury, a beautiful 48-acre Episcopal retreat center in Oviedo, Florida, to what promised to be a historic gathering between Jews and Christians led by Rabbi Zalman Schachter-Shalomi. It was just months before my rabbinic ordination, so I was especially eager to observe my mentor interacting with Christians in an intimate, weekend-long retreat. Reb Zalman was co-leading with Father Edward G. Zogby, who was vice president of Fordham University in New York City. The retreat was called "Dance around the Midnight Pole; Happy Birthday, Jesus"—a title typical of the wry humor and fearless innovation that Reb Zalman always brought to his work.

On the Eastern Orthodox, Catholic, Anglican, and Lutheran calendars, January 1 became a special holiday called the Feast of the Circumcision. Count eight days from December 25, the day Jesus's birthday is celebrated, and you arrive at January 1, the date Christian tradition assigns to Jesus's ritual circumcision (*brit milah*). The day we celebrate the secular New Year is actually a commemoration for Christians of Jesus's first religious ritual as a Jew. Reb Zalman had proposed this Sabbath retreat many months before, planning to use the sacred technology of the Passover seder to enhance the celebration of the New Year at midnight on Saturday. He believed a commemoration of Jesus's *brit milah* on New Year's Eve would offset the secular tradition of a party based on merriment and drinking.

The plan was that on Saturday afternoon the Jews would teach the Christians the structure of the Passover seder: the four questions, the telling of the Exodus story, four glasses of wine, a festive meal, and lots of singing. In this retreat, though, the story told would be about the birth of Jesus, and how the Gospels helped change the world. The four questions would relate to Jesus's life, and the four cups of wine and festive meal would be integrated into a formal Catholic Mass commemorating the body, heart, mind, and the spirit of Jesus indwelling in every Christian. The Mass itself would begin at midnight, followed by an all-night study, prayer, and meditation vigil in the manner of the Eastern Orthodox Church. The vigil would culminate with a traditional Jewish morning worship service at sunrise led by Reb Zalman.

There were approximately two hundred participants—Jews, Catholics, Episcopalians, and Methodists. After welcoming the Sabbath with traditional blessings over the candles, wine, and bread, Friday evening was spent chanting and singing songs from the Psalms in Hebrew, Latin, and English led by Reb Zalman and Father Zogby. It was magnificent. But after a long day of traveling we retired early knowing that the next day would be mysterious, long, and filled with surprises. We would not be disappointed.

After a morning service of Jewish prayers and Catholic chants, Reb Zalman read from the Torah portion that describes Moses's intimate encounter with God at the burning bush. This was followed by deep teachings from Reb Zalman and Father Zogby on the Jewishness of Jesus and the birth of Christianity. We were then asked to take some time alone to contemplate how we might overlay the template of the Passover seder onto the story of Jesus's birth in a way that was authentic and respectful of the key differences in each of our religions. We all sensed the historic nature of the weekend. This was clearly not just a meeting with brothers and sisters of another faith, but an unexpected encounter between ourselves and God.

When we gathered again in the afternoon it was time for the Jews to teach the Christians about the structure of the seder and how we blend rituals and symbols into the telling of the Exodus story. Then the Christians would collaborate with us on how to incorporate the story of Jesus into their own Haggadah (a booklet that tells the story) that would be read that night as part of the Midnight Mass. Of course, the sacred task of creating an authentic Christian seder took many hours. We had a light dinner together and retired to our own rooms for rest, knowing that our Midnight Mass with seder would last until sunrise.

When we came together at 11:30 PM it was with a sense of anticipation and awe. We knew that in the 2,000-year history of the church and the synagogue, no rabbi or priest had dared to create this kind of ceremony. This was not a hybrid or fusion, but rather a "new thing" like the prophets Isaiah and Jeremiah had spoken about, lending one religion's template to the telling of another religion's sacred story.

We started slowly, easing into the ritual with Hebrew songs from the Psalms, as we had the night before. At midnight Father Zogby, who by that time we were addressing affectionately as Father Ed, began leading the Mass. Our role as Jews was not to participate, but to be sacred witnesses to the ceremony of our Christian friends. At Reb Zalman's request the Mass was chanted in Latin with line-by-line English translations.

> Father Ed: *In nomine Patris, et Filii, et Spiritus Sancti.* In the name of
> the Father, the Son, and the Holy Spirit.
> Christians: *Amen.*

The Mass continued with the doxology known as *Gloria in excelsis Deo,* a powerful ceremony of confession, and then we reached the canon.

> Father Ed: *Dominus vobiscum.* May the Lord be with you.
> Christians: *Et cum spiritu tuo.* And also with you.
> Father Ed: *Sursum corda.* Lift up your hearts.
> Christians. *Habemus ad Dominum.* We lift them up to the Lord.
> Father Ed: *Gratias agamus Domino Deo nostro.* Let us give thanks
> to the Lord our God.
> Christians: *Dignum et iustum est.* It is right to give thanks and
> praise.

Then Father Ed fell silent. He had been leading the service in Latin from memory with no missal (prayer book) in his hands. The silence grew until everyone knew something was wrong; the priest didn't know what came next. There was a kind of collective bewilderment as we waited for him to recover. It occurred to me since he was now an administrative priest at Fordham, he wasn't leading Mass on a daily, or even a weekly, basis. This could be a long pause.

Suddenly another voice rang out, *"Pax Domini sit semper vobiscum.* May the peace of the Lord be always with you." We all stared as Reb Zalman, sitting next to Father Zogby, smoothly supplied the next line. The Catholics chanted back, *"Et cum spiritu tuo.* And also with you." It was as if the whole room let out a breath of relief, and then we all laughed at the wild wonder of this moment.

The evening continued with the reading of the new Haggadah the Christians had created to tell their story. It was glorious and unforgettable, but what stood out most in all our minds was the miraculous instant when the rabbi sang out during the Mass to help his friend, the priest.

Later that night, I leaned over to Reb Zalman and asked, "How did you know what to say?" He explained that decades earlier he'd memorized large portions of the Mass in Latin as a tribute to his deep respect for Catholicism beginning in the 1950s and his personal friendship with Thomas Merton, with whom he used to take summer retreats at the Abbey of Gethsemani in Kentucky in the 1960s. With a twinkle in his eye he leaned in and whispered, *"Baruch Hashem!* Blessed is God! It sure came in handy tonight!" I laughed, feeling grateful again to have this courageous, once-in-a-generation rabbi as my teacher. The weekend ended with a sunrise service in Hebrew, and as we left on January 1, we said goodbye to each other with *"Shana tova,* Happy New Year."

A Seder for Tibet

In 1990, my teacher Rabbi Zalman Schachter-Shalomi was invited to travel with a small delegation of religious Jewish leaders to meet the Dalai Lama, spiritual leader of the Tibetan Buddhists, at his home-in-exile, Dharmasala, India. The Dalai Lama realized that the Jewish people had secrets for surviving for generations in exile, which he hoped to apply to his own people's situation. Tibet had been brutally invaded by the People's Republic of China in 1949 and occupied ever since, resulting in more than a million deaths and repression of Tibetan Buddhist practices. In 1959, the Dalai Lama fled his homeland and was welcomed by India to establish a government-in-exile there.

Rabbi Zalman knew the Passover seder was one of the "secrets" that had helped maintain Jewish dignity and hope during the long exile from our homeland in Israel. He hoped to share the framework of the Passover ceremony so that the Tibetans could create their own seder to use in family ceremonies each year, just as Jews do every spring on Passover.

Poet and author Rodger Kamenetz accompanied the group of Jewish leaders to document this historic trip. Later, in his acclaimed book *The Jew in the Lotus*,[125] Kamenetz writes that Reb Zalman "proposed to give to the Buddhists the 'shell' of a ceremony in which they could insert their own program, a seder built around the life of Buddha, four cups of wine, one for each stage of his enlightenment."

Although the new ceremony didn't happen on the first trip to Dharmasala, Kamenetz returned in 1996 to fulfill Reb Zalman's dream of creating a structure for the Tibetans based on the Passover ceremony. Kamenetz says Reb Zalman believed that the Tibetan "emigrants living in India or the United States would lose their culture unless new family ceremonies were created for the exile situation. He saw the seder not as an old Bentley, but as a survival vehicle—one that Tibetan families could customize."[126]

Kamenetz told the Dalai Lama,

We are going to celebrate soon—at the next full moon—
Passover. It's a celebration of freedom, when the Jews left
Egypt, where they were slaves. We have a tradition that
every nation is included and ultimately will be freed, and we
certainly pray each year that Tibet will be free. . . . At the end
we say, "Next Year in Jerusalem." I believe some Tibetans once
hung a banner in Dharmasala that said, "Next Year in Lhasa."

The Dalai Lama replied,

After we came to India we learned how the Jewish community,
the Jewish people, carried the struggle in different parts of the
world and under difficult circumstances through such a long
period; then we were very much affected. In the early sixties
we often used to mention how we have to learn something of
the Jewish secrets to preserve your identity and your culture
and to develop it—in some cases, in hostile surroundings—
over the centuries. So now we also use "Next year in Lhasa";
I think that also we learned. We are copying your practice.[127]

Kamenetz reports that the Dalai Lama smiled broadly after he spoke.

Later that week a small group of Tibetans, including the learned monk
Geshe Sonam Rinchen and some prominent American Jewish-American
Buddhists (affectionately called JuBus), attended the seder that Kamenetz
organized. He told those assembled, "So at the *Pesakh* seder, you yourself
are being freed, not just people in the past. And because this promise will
extend to all people, of freedom, we choose a psalm of freedom from
captivity. We are reading it for the people of Tibet."[128] Kamenetz then read
a line he adapted from Psalm 126:1, "When the Holy One will return the
captivity of Zion/Tibet, we will be like dreamers. Then our mouths will be

filled with laughter. The Holy One has done great things. Those who sow in tears will reap in joy." After the reading he saw a tear in Geshe Sonam's eye as the words were translated to him. Kamenetz finished his account of the seder with these words of wisdom:

> Paradoxically, by sharing the seder this way, donating part of it to other peoples, we begin to see the value of it more clearly for ourselves. In this time of pluralism, we Jews don't have to fear. Our tradition will only become more beautiful as we share it with others. No longer something to hold tightly and defensively to ourselves, our tradition is becoming what it was meant to be, foretold to Abraham so long ago: a blessing to humanity and a gift to bestow with open arms.[129]

The seder that Reb Zalman envisioned in 1990 came full-circle when the Dalai Lama himself attended a large seder in Washington, DC, in 1997 with dignitaries and Jewish leaders, including Supreme Court justice Stephen Breyer. The event was conceived by Kamenetz, who organized a nationwide campaign to inspire Jews to become involved with the struggle for Tibetan freedom. The idea spread throughout the country. My own congregation in Oregon, along with many synagogues throughout the country, participated that year in "seders for Tibet." In a letter to the participants of these seders, the Dalai Lama sent this inspiring message:

> In our dialogue with rabbis and Jewish scholars, the Tibetan people have learned about the secrets of Jewish spiritual survival in exile: one secret is the Passover seder. Through it, for 2,000 years, even in very difficult times, Jewish people remember their liberation from slavery to freedom and this has brought you hope in times of difficulty. We are grateful to our Jewish brothers and sisters for adding to their celebration of freedom the thought of freedom for the Tibetan people.[130]

Pentecost: A Poem

Passover and Easter:
two moon-linked sisters
who long ago stopped speaking,
yet each linked to the fullness of our hearts,
and the fullness of God's grace.
The moon of Sister Miriam desires freedom
and the rescue of her people
from the cruelty of Pharaoh,
by the outstretched, mighty hand of the Lord:
a hand of salvation reaching down from heaven,
and passing through my nation,
and down through yours,
and then to each and every one of us—
so may it be!
The moon of Mother Mary desires to give her light
so that each man and woman
may know the power of the resurrection,
and the soil of death
that holds the seeds of rebirth within:
a resurrection reaching upward,
passing through all nations
and up to God Almighty!
Two celebrations: two women: Miriam and Mary,
who don't even know they have the same name—
one in Hebrew and one in Greek—
yet linked to a single full moon.
And then we each begin to count:
we both count to fifty—
beyond the forty days

of Moses on Mt. Sinai

and Jesus in the wilderness.

We go beyond, one cycle further:

to fifty, Shavuot, the Pentecost.

Ours to the revelation of Torah at Sinai.

Yours to the revelation of the Holy Spirit.

Freedom and resurrection.

Revelation and revelation.

Twelve tribes and twelve disciples.

One moon, two traditions.

Two covenants, one God.

Shavuot and Pentecost:

two cousins

who have just begun to speak.

And King David sings to us

from his tomb today:

"Teach us to count our days

that we may open our hearts to Your Wisdom."

Some of us, thank God, are listening!

A Catholic Seder

Just before Passover in 2014, my friend Father Mike Walker of Shepherd of the Valley Catholic Church in southern Oregon asked me: "How do you feel about Christians holding seders in their churches?"

I answered honestly, "I don't think it's a good idea."

Father Mike nodded. "What's the problem?"

"Well, the way Christian seders are usually presented is a misappropriation of a Jewish ritual."

I explained that the church seders I knew about took Jewish symbols and gave them Christological meaning. For example, the stripes on the matzah are said to represent the stripes from the whipping that Jesus received at the hand of the Romans; the broken middle matzah symbolizes Jesus's brokenness. In a Jewish seder, we hide the larger part of the middle matzah, and the children have to search for it and return it to the adults after dinner so that the seder can be completed. At one of these so-called Christian seders, it was explained that Jesus was the hidden part of the matzah, and the meal of life can only be completed when he is returned. These examples are definitely not Jewish tradition—and they are hurtful examples of replacement theology.

"There is enough richness and deep meaning in your Eucharist that you don't have to imitate the Jewish Passover ritual at the church," I told him. "You could have a model seder with a meal but without the sacred blessings that Jews say in a regular Passover seder. That would be authentic and respectful."

"Fine," he said. "Will you lead a model seder for us this year?"

I laughed, "Well, I guess I got myself into that one!"

I prepared a special handout to use as a Haggadah (the booklet with prayers and songs for a seder). In it were explanations of the ritual items on the seder plate, the story of the liberation of the Hebrew slaves, and interpretations on the relevance in our lives today. At the seder we discussed the meaning of the symbols and story, and we sang some traditional Passover songs. We enjoyed the ritual four cups of wine, the matzah, and the bitter herbs followed by a simple meal.

This year, a few months before I was to conduct my third seder for Father Mike's church, I got a call from Francis, the church's volunteer chef. "I'd like to serve lamb at the seder," he said. Two years earlier, before our first seder, Francis had confided to me that he thought Jews still slaughtered lambs for our Passover meals. I explained we haven't done that since biblical times, in favor of foods like matzoh ball soup, chicken, and brisket, which have become the traditional seder fare. Because of the complexity of kosher dietary rules, though, I had him serve salmon as their main dish for the first two seders. But now he wanted to serve lamb again.

"Why?" I asked.

"Well, I think that for us it can represent the Paschal Lamb from the Jewish Passover, and Jesus being called the Lamb of God in Christianity."

This made sense, and I was intrigued. "Okay," I told him. "I'll see what I can do."

I found a rancher in our area who raises organically fed sheep, and slaughters and sells lambs each spring. The chef arranged to have two lambs slaughtered in a kosher manner, their meat butchered and cubed. When I arrived at the seder, the chef pulled me aside to show me the special seder plate at my table. Each table had a ritual plate with parsley, saltwater, horseradish, hard-boiled egg, a fruit and nut mixture called *charoset*, and a shank bone.

He said, "This shank bone is from one of the lambs we slaughtered." Even though I knew he'd bought the lamb from the rancher I'd recommended, my jaw dropped.

"I've gone to seders all my life," I said, "but I've never seen a shank bone from a lamb that I was responsible for having slaughtered."

As I sat and stared at the bone, I pictured the lamb, and my heart opened. I had never felt connected to a shank bone before. Suddenly I realized this living being had given its life so we could have a special meal for our seder. All of the other symbols on the plate seemed to rise into sharper focus, revolving around the bone. As we ate the beautifully slow-cooked meat together, I imagined I could still feel the traces of the lamb's short life. It seemed like we were participating in an ancient rite of communion.

Later in the week I described my experience to Father Mike as we compared notes about the seder. We agreed that using the shank bone and eating that lamb offered a new dimension to both the Paschal Lamb the Jews read about during Passover, and the Lamb of God the Christians commemorate in the Lord's Supper.

I took the shank bone home from the seder and kept it in my refrigerator. Later that month it graced my family's seder plate, and then our synagogue's community seder. When I shared the story of the lamb with both family and community, we took time to pause, gaze at the shank bone, and think of that very lamb. All the voices around the seder table were deeper and more resonant as we prayed, thanking both God and the soul of the innocent animal that was slaughtered.

Reimagining Exodus—A Conclusion

The stories of the Exodus unfold until each of us comes to our own astonishing discovery—that our personal stories are, in a mysterious way, retellings of the Exodus stories; that our lives relive the lives of our ancestors. Part of our role in the covenant is to get right what our ancestors got wrong. In Judaism we call this two-step process *tikkun hanefesh* ("repairing the soul") and *tikkun olam* ("repairing the world"). We repair ourselves in order to help repair our world.

Most of the Exodus stories don't "preachify" with pronouncements like "freedom is good, slavery is bad." In each of the episodes, we get to witness God's interactions with Moses and the people, and the people's interactions with each other. Most of the commandments for holy living are found in Leviticus. Wisdom teachings are found in Proverbs and Ecclesiastes. But in Exodus, the moral of each story is left for each of us to wrestle with, interpret, and apply to our own lives today.

If we hope to find a model of perfect human behavior in the Elder and Younger Testaments stories, we won't find it. Except for Jesus in Christianity, all the heroes in the Bible are flawed: from Adam and Eve, to Noah, Abraham and Sarah, to Tamar, Rebecca, Rachel, Moses, and David, to all of Jesus's disciples. What so many of us love about biblical characters like Moses and King David is that we can relate to them. They wear their emotions on their sleeves; we see their mistakes, and they remind us of ourselves—the way we want to be, and the way we don't want to be.

The Bible offers us perfect stories about imperfect people. Even Moses, as humble and brilliant as he was, is very human. He has fits of rage, self-doubt, and moments of deep despair. Yet in the most significant way, Moses is not like anyone else in the Bible, nor is he really like any of us. His dialogues recorded in the Torah are not with his rabbi, therapist, best friend, men's group, or wife. We learn about all his emotional experiences from his one-on-one, back-and-forth conversations with none other than the Creator of the universe. Moses is not in the model of a sinless Jesus or Muhammad, or an enlightened Buddha, but after the theophany at the burning bush, he too lives at a transcendent level—just beyond our reach. No person in history has risen to such an exalted level of consciousness as Moses, who knew God face to face, and who saw the deep interconnection between spiritual awakening and political freedom.

Even though we may aspire to be more like any of the founders of these great religions, very few of us, if any, make the choices they made that led them to become what they were. Our spiritual traditions offer us more than biographies of lone, heroic figures. We have human beings embedded into stories—complex stories woven with the threads of failure, then success, then betrayal, then an even greater success. And these characters woven into the arc of the stories mirror our own lives.

There is a reason the Exodus story is so well known throughout the world: it is accessible. People in any culture can relate to the failures and successes of the Hebrews. The saga of Moses and the children of Israel is more than 3,000 years old, yet it is constantly being renewed, reimagined, and made relevant. It's about a particular group of people, in a particular place, and in a particular time in history, yet dozens of groups and religious denominations have described themselves as "Israel." There is little doubt that the Exodus story is the most influential liberation story ever told, and will likely continue to be so. Its stars, co-stars, and cast of thousands are flawed heroes and complex villains, and we see ourselves in them.

The Exodus does what a good mirror does: it reflects the light back upon the looker. May we all be blessed by the Holy One of Israel to continue gazing and reflecting upon the Exodus stories until we are each personally free, and until the entire world is liberated from every kind of oppression and injustice imaginable. We also pray that the Exodus story of the Jewish people will never be misappropriated and used to justify anti-Semitism, racism, prejudice of any kind, tyranny, and injustice.

Finally, I am thankful to God that the Jewish people were chosen to be the custodians of such an epic story that has brought so much inspiration and hope to so many people over the ages.

APPENDICES

Some Names of God

Almighty, Lord of Hosts, and the God Who Sees

When God is named by people, or when God makes known a name to someone, that name reveals a unique aspect of the divine character. Abraham knew God as *El Shaddai*, translated as "God Almighty." The Hebrew root of *Shaddai* is uncertain, but it is probably related to either *shod* meaning "breast" or *sodeh* meaning "field." It is possible that this name originally referred to God's feminine or nurturing aspect, through breast-like nurturance or the fecundity of the earth.

To Hannah, God appeared as *YHVH Tz'vaote*, usually translated as "Lord of Hosts" (1 Sam. 1:11). The English word *host* is now archaic except for the host of a party, a restaurant host who seats people, and the consecrated bread at church. In the thirteenth century, though, the word meant "a multitude," and that is the meaning of the Hebrew word it translated. It can also be rendered as "array," like the constellations in the sky, or an organized military formation.

To Hagar, God appeared as *El-roi*, which literally means "God Who Sees" or "God Who Sees Me," since the Holy One saw her anguish when Sarah dealt harshly with her. *El* refers to God as the "Mighty One," and *roi* means "sees me." The Torah says, "So she named the LORD who spoke to her, 'You are El-roi'; for she said, 'Have I really seen God and remained alive after seeing him?'" (Gen. 16:13).

Lord, Jehovah, and Being

Moses doesn't give God a name, but God teaches Moses the special divine title known as the Tetragrammaton: "I appeared to Abraham, Isaac, and Jacob as God Almighty, but by my name 'The LORD' I did not make myself known to them" (Exod. 6:3). The poor English translations "The LORD" has little to do with the Hebrew. The word is spelled *yod hey vav hey*—YHVH (or YHWH) using English letters—hence Tetragrammaton meaning four-letter name. In more and more contemporary Jewish translations of the Torah, this name is written as YHVH since it is so challenging to translate into English.

The letters YHVH spell out the past, present, and future tenses of the word for being: was, is, and will be. It could be interpreted as the Holy One of Being, or even Self-Existent One. YHVH is the most commonly used divine appellation in the Tanakh, used more than 6,500 times. English translations should use the word Being, or something similar, since God specifically told Moses at the burning bush: "This is my name forever, and this my title for all generations." When Jesus teaches his disciples the Lord's Prayer, "Our Father in heaven, hallowed be your name" (Matt. 6:9), the word "name" almost certainly refers to the Tetragrammaton—the name of God that refers to God's presence and imminence within creation. *Jehovah* is a transliteration of this divine name, although there is no letter "j" in Hebrew.

Just as with the English word *being*, YHVH can be thought of as both active as a verb and solid as a noun. All Hebrew nouns, like those in many other languages, are either masculine or feminine, and as a noun YHVH is feminine. It simply cannot be accurately translated as "LORD." For whatever reason, the early translators chose not to translate this divine name literally, and so it came into English as "LORD" based on the Greek *Kyrios* and the Latin *Dominus* (Septuagint and Vulgate), both of which have to do with domineering or lordship, not being.

Is it possible that the translators were uncomfortable with the abstract, feminine meaning of YHVH? Perhaps they assumed people needed the hierarchal and powerful name of "LORD." However, biblical Hebrew has the word *Adon*, which means "LORD" or "Master," which is used to address God or an esteemed person. The Tetragrammaton is almost the opposite of "LORD"; it implies that God is imminent and close to every person and thing in creation.

First-century Jewish philosopher Philo of Alexandria was renowned for his allegorical interpretations of the Tanakh. He understood how challenging it was to name an unlimited Deity with a name that by its nature is limited. He suggests that at the burning bush God told Moses the following:

> "I Am That I Am" which is equivalent to saying, "It is my nature to be, not to be described by name, but in order that the human race may not be wholly destitute of any appellation which they may give to the most excellent of beings, I allow you to use the word Lord as a name; the Lord God of three natures—of instruction, and of holiness, and of the practice of virtue; of which Abraham, and Isaac, and Jacob are recorded as the symbols."[131]

What's in a Name?

The proper nouns (place names and personal names) used in the Tanakh offer insights into history that are revealed through etymological study of "the Hebrew language"—insights that get lost in translating the Bible into any language. Historically, it is possible that some of the place names in the Exodus saga did not have the same meanings that we are reading into them today. This does not mean that many of the sites were named without conscious intent. Some already existed as Egyptian villages and desert oases; others may have been named by the Semitic Hyksos who called various locations by names that seem to be Hebraic. Many of the place names were probably given by the Hebrews who had been freed from slavery, and who were now journeying back to their ancestral homeland. What we know about ancient Semitic peoples, based on clear anecdotal evidence from the Bible, is that the root metaphors discovered in the etymology of proper nouns were seen as very important. In Genesis 2:19, for example, we learn that God brings the animals and birds to Adam so he could name him. One of the greatest gifts God gives to Adam, in fact, is the power of language—the power to name that which is around him.

We may name our children "Sophia" or "James" but we may not know much about the origin of the name. In the Bible, when a place, a person, or even God is named, that name and its meaning were given consciously. After the birth of each of Jacob's twelve sons, a clear reason is given for each name.[132] For example, when Leah named her son Reuben, the name had the celebratory meaning of "See, A Son!" When she named her handmaid Zilpah's son Gad, she felt God had brought her good fortune, which is what his name means in Hebrew: "And Leah said, 'Good fortune!' so she named him Gad" (Gen. 30:11).

In the same sense, the Hebrews were very conscious of how and why they assigned specific names to places. When Abimelech and

Abraham made an oath together, the Torah says: "Therefore that place was called Beer-sheba; because there both of them swore an oath" (Gen. 21:31). One way to translate the name *Beer Sheva* is "well of oaths." There are many other place names in the Bible named for the specific nature of the event that took place there.[133]

The Reason for the Season

There is an organic flow between all of the Jewish holidays that mirrors the cycles in nature. In the Creation story, we learn that "there was evening and there was morning, the first day" (Gen. 1:5). Jews continue to mark the beginning of the day at sunset—evening—and not at midnight as most of the world does. Just as the calendar begins each day in the evening, so the New Year begins in the "evening of the seasons," autumn with the celebration of Rosh Hashannah (the New Year) and Yom Kippur (the Day of Atonement). Six months later in the "morning of the seasons," the spring, Jews celebrate the festivals of Purim and Passover. Each of these festivals has a direct connection to its season.

Seasonal affective disorder (SAD) is a form of depression experienced by some people in winter. However, all people are emotionally impacted by the cycle of seasons. We tend to feel more introspective in the autumn, more reclusive in winter, more liberated in spring, and more outgoing in summer. Seasonal effects are made sacred in many religions, especially ones that developed in temperate climates. In most religions, the seasons and sacred holidays are strongly aligned.

The Jewish spiritual system of holy days and festivals is organic— each part arises from a particular season, and each part is connected to the year as a whole. As an individual enters into the spring season of vitality and liberation, the intensely self-reflective work of Yom Kippur would not be appropriate, just as remembering our liberation at the Passover seder wouldn't be organic in September.

In 1995 when I was ordained, my teacher Rabbi Zalman Schachter-Shalomi invited me to assist him at a multi-day retreat he was doing in Rio de Janeiro in Brazil. I remember getting on the plane in Oregon in early September when autumn was in the air. The sense of nature falling back upon itself was imminent, and along with that came the biological sense that it was time to do the self-reflective work Judaism prescribes for that time of year. We all know that when it's autumn in the United States, it's springtime south of the equator, so when I got off the plane the feeling in the air was that of springtime liberation. It was a startling contrast; in a fifteen-hour plane ride I traveled six months into the future, from autumn to spring. God's immanence where I live in the Northwest was calling for introspection whereas God in Brazil at that same moment was calling for freedom and liberation.

Both Judaism and Christianity evolved in temperate climates in the northern hemisphere, so it's only natural that both Passover and Easter would occur during springtime. So, I was in Rio de Janeiro in September but the feeling was of Passover and Easter. Both religions there have lost their organic, seasonal mooring by conforming to the historical times to celebrate each holiday in the northern hemisphere. On Sunday morning of the gathering in Rio, Reb Zalman challenged several dozen rabbis and spiritual leaders from Jewish communities throughout South America to consider celebrating the Jewish holidays at a time of the year that was authentic and natural to where they were living. In other words, they would celebrate Passover in September and Yom Kippur in April.

This would be comparable to Christians south of the equator celebrating Christmas in June and Easter in September. Reb Zalman humorously told the group, "I have an opinion but I don't live here so I don't get a vote. Take one hundred years or so before you make a decision, but it's a worthy discussion to have." People laughed, but a serious discussion really did begin after that gathering. There is a feeling in every season, and our holidays—and our emotions—are intimately linked to the effect of the season.

Theodicy: Divine Providence and the Existence of Evil

Passover and Easter both recall the good that came out of evil—the liberation of the Hebrews after enslavement in Egypt and the resurrection of Jesus after his crucifixion by Rome. Both holidays have political liberation and social freedom at their foundations. For Judaism, it was the Jewish people's liberation from subjugation under the rule of Pharaoh. For Christianity, the same Jewish people were occupied by the Roman Empire, whose rulers were concerned that a messiah would arise from among the people and lead a fight for independence.

Jesus was not crucified because of his spiritual teachings. Rather, he was perceived to be a political threat to Rome, whose leaders knew that in first-century Judea, the idea of a messiah had explicit political implications. The emperor of Rome and his appointed governor of Judea would likely have heard of prophesies, such as, "For a child has been born for us . . . authority rests upon his shoulders" (Isa. 9:6). They feared the popular unrest that had been present in Judea since the beginning of the Roman occupation around 37 BCE. They knew that the citizens of Judea wanted independence and yearned for a time when "a king will reign in righteousness, and princes will rule with justice" (Isa. 32:1). And the Romans knew that the Jewish people thought of such a king as a messiah, a spiritual leader as well as a political and military leader.

To fully understand the parallels of Exodus and the Cross, we need to recognize that Rabbinic Judaism and Christianity are sibling religions, and both are formed from stories that can be viewed as colossal failures. Jesus, the centralizing focus of the new religion, was crucified by the Romans around 36 CE just outside the walls of Jerusalem. The Temple of Solomon, the centralizing focus for Jews at that time, was destroyed by the Romans in 70 CE within those same walls. These two events, taking place within a few decades and a few hundred meters of each other, would become pivotal in the development of each religion, emerging out of what seemed to be failure.

After the temple's destruction, the centralized priesthood of the Sadducees was forced to yield control to the decentralized local rabbis, the Pharisees. The creative genius of the Pharisees is the main reason Judaism survived the destruction of the temple. They transmuted the traditional system of bringing offerings to the temple in Jerusalem into a system in which prayer itself would be acceptable as an offering.

Likewise, Christianity took the tragedy of the Cross and transformed it into a religion based on the idea that out of death comes resurrection, out of suffering new life can emerge. In both cases, "failure" led to renewal. Nevertheless, one wonders why God uses suffering—crucifixion, slavery, despotic regimes, failure, and evil—to bring hope, freedom, liberation, and forgiveness. Why does evil exist? How can a loving God permit the innocent to suffer? For answers, we look to a branch of theology called "theodicy."

Theodicy is the philosophical quest to justify the existence of a sovereign God with the simultaneous existence of evil. Both Judaism and Christianity are confronted with the dilemma that Rabbi Harold Kushner summed up in asking "why bad things happen to good people."[134] Why would God permit the pharaohs of Egypt and the emperors of Rome to oppress the Jewish people? Out of these philosophical ponderings come two different but parallel responses. At the center of each is a liberation story: one overtly political and the other overtly spiritual.

Two of Judaism's founders, Abraham and Moses, wrestled with God around understanding why innocent people are allowed to suffer. When witnessing the destruction of Sodom, Abraham courageously argues with God, asking, "Will you indeed sweep away the righteous with the wicked?" (Gen. 18:23). Regarding the suffering of the Hebrew slaves, Moses questions God's motives when he asks, "Why have you mistreated this people?" (Exod. 5:22).

The great thirteenth-century Jewish philosopher and physician Rabbi Moses ben Nachman Girondi, known as Nachmanides, acknowledges that the problem of evil is "the most difficult matter which is at the root both of faith and of disbelief, with which scholars of all ages, people and tongues have struggled."[135] No theologian in any faith tradition has ever adequately explained why God permits evil to exist and why the innocent suffer. We can explore the interface of these central stories of suffering and liberation within Judaism and Christianity, asking the hard questions and considering again the different ways in which they are answered.

1. Mystery

For some, divine providence is synonymous with fate or destiny, even predestination. However, in Judaism, divine providence refers to God's purpose, design, and involvement in the natural world in every moment and in every detail of existence. Divine providence means that the way every leaf falls to the ground, where it lands, the angle at which it sits on the ground, every rustling movement it makes, every insect that climbs upon it, and what happens to it at every stage of its decay is fated, designed, and overseen by God at every moment. Everything about that leaf's existence and eventual decay is within the scope of divine providence. But is this the same thing as fate?

In Psalm 139:4, King David expresses the notion of providence and predestination when he chants: "Even before a word is on my tongue, O LORD, you know it completely." King David was saying that God knows not only our thoughts in the present, but also what we are going to say in the future. The New Living Translation of the Bible renders this verse as, "You know what I am going to say even before I say it, LORD." Such a radical view of providential design has the net effect of eliminating any real distinction between free will and predestination.

The Baal Shem Tov takes it a step further by eliminating the distinction between nature and miracles. In his view, every natural occurrence is a miracle because God has intervened in the occurrence at every point in time and space. The only difference between nature and a miracle is that the miracle is something you see for the first time. The first time you see a flower bloom, you perceive it as a miracle. After the second and third time, you start expecting it and say it's nature. There is no difference, says the Baal Shem Tov, between the parting of the Red Sea and the sun rising every morning.

But then we come up against the nature of evil. Once we accept divine providence, we are forced to ask: If the one true God is involved in all aspects of existence, why permit despots to commit horrible acts? If God is involved in every detail of creation, does God participate in evil actions? If divine providence is taken seriously, these questions cannot be dodged. Why did the Hebrews have to suffer in slavery? Why did Jesus have to suffer on the cross? All theistic religions attempt to address the question by using what I call "the mystery defense." We might say God uses it with the prophet Isaiah: "For my thoughts are not your thoughts, nor are your ways my ways, says the LORD" (Isa. 55:8).

One of Judaism's greatest teachers, the twelfth-century philosopher Maimonides, does his best to try to resolve this puzzle of predestination and free will, but in the end he too falls back on the mystery defense. He writes:

> The Holy One knows everything that will happen before it happens. Does He know whether a particular person will be righteous or wicked, or not? If He does know, then it will be impossible for that person not to be righteous. If He knows that he will be righteous but that it is possible for him to be wicked, then He does not know everything that He has created . . . *we do not have the capabilities to comprehend how the Holy One, Blessed Be He, knows all creations and events.* Know, without a

doubt, that people do what they want without the Holy One forcing or decreeing upon them to do so.[136]

The best our theologians can do is to say that God does not commit the evil per se but gives people the free will to choose between good deeds or evil deeds. The logic works to some degree in certain circumstances. But mass murder? The Holocaust? Rape? Child abuse? We are forced to ask why God does not intervene in these circumstances to stop the atrocities. The theological justification tends to go something like this: God has given humanity free will. If God intervenes whenever an evil act is being committed, then there really is no free will. Therefore, it is humanity's responsibility to intervene and stop heinous behavior.

For example, the question concerning the Holocaust becomes not "Where was God?" but rather, "Where were people?" And why did humanity not intervene in Armenia? Germany? Rwanda? Syria? Judaism says that God and the angels weep with every victim. Christianity says that Jesus suffers along with the suffering. Is this too part of the mystery, that divine providence leads God to weep over what must happen?

2. *The Trial of God*

Elie Wiesel's play *The Trial of God* was inspired by an actual trial he witnessed as a young man. After the liberation of Auschwitz, a trial was called by the most pious, religious leaders in the camp. God was accused of breaking the covenant he made with the Jewish people. Wiesel reports that "the outcome did not go well. God was found guilty." He concludes by telling us that after the trial, these same men then began their afternoon prayers to the same God they had just found guilty. In a strange way, there is a measure of satisfaction for us in Wiesel's story. Why? Because it does not rely on the helpless mystery argument. Nor does it deny God's responsibility. Nor does it offer a clever, mind-bending paradox that takes intellectual gymnastics to comprehend.

It is ironic that putting God on trial after the Holocaust actually confirmed faith in God for this group of religious Jews. The Holocaust breached the covenantal agreement of being a chosen people. It had gone further than Isaiah's vision of Israel as a suffering servant. Theological platitudes are not enough after the Holocaust. The trial that Wiesel reports to us, as painful as it must have been to witness, actually gave the most pious believers a reason to maintain their faith. That's why these men were able to continue praying.

The suggestion that a natural disaster, in which human behavior is not a factor, is part of divine providence is also unsettling. Gone is the argument that God is respecting the free will of humans to do what is right or not. In legal parlance, natural disasters are called "acts of God." The mystic often focuses on the beauty in the world of the Divine dance and not the catastrophe. It's wonderful to imagine the Divine involved in the falling of every leaf, the direction of every breeze, in the tiniest whirl of every atom at every moment. But this view of God is limited unless decay, death, sin, and disaster are taken into account.

How can we avoid side-stepping the question by saying it's all a mystery? The next step is often dualism—seeing the spiritual world as comprised of a god of evil and a god of good.

3. *Dualism*

In the evolution of human religion, it is logical to imagine the deification of an independent, negative force that competes with the goodness of God. Dualism seems to be based in our neurobiology. The rhythms of breath and heartbeat, and other bodily functions, lend themselves to perceiving the world as possessing independent oppositional forces—a god of life and a god of death; a god of summer and a god of winter. The mind naturally distinguishes the healthy from the unhealthy; pleasure from pain; that which promotes survival and that which threatens survival. Dualism, on the other hand, a god of goodness and a separate god of evil, is not consistent with Jewish, Christian, or Islamic theologies.

Absolute dualism asserts that the two forces of good and evil coexist in a balance of power—one does not come before the other. Historically, some form of Gnostic dualism has been the most common response to the issue of God permitting evil: God represents good, and some kind of Satan or satanic force represents the evil power. But the dualistic premise of Gnosticism is unacceptable within traditional Judaism, Christianity, and Islam. What theologians call mitigated dualism, which sees evil as subordinate to good, is intrinsic to the philosophies of all three monotheistic faiths. For instance, we see a trace of it in the mainstream Jewish notion that everyone is born with two—the inclination to do good, *yetzer tov*, and the inclination to do evil, *yetzer hara*.

Monotheism describes God as sovereign and in absolute control of both good and evil. In the book of Job, for example, Satan has no autonomous power but must ask for and receive permission from God to test Job's faith. Satan cannot act independently of God. This returns us, then, to the age-old question: how can a sovereign deity allow all the evil we see in the world? God's disturbing statement about this is translated in the King James Bible as "I make peace, and create evil" (Isa. 45:7). In the early centuries of the Common Era, the rabbis were concerned about the dualism that could arise if people grappled with the idea that God creates evil. They side-stepped the issue by changing the wording to "makes peace, and creates *all things*" in Jewish prayerbooks.

Intellectually, every religion has been subject to the influence of dualism, since it is the only argument that keeps us from thinking of God as participating in evil in some way. It is, indeed, very challenging for a monotheist to make an intellectual argument that explains how a God of justice permits evil to exist, let alone that an omniscient God who knows in advance that an evil act or natural disaster is going to occur does nothing to stop it.

4. Monism

Putting aside the issue of evil for a moment, once we accept the notion of God's imminence in all of creation, it is intellectually difficult to draw a line where this imminence might logically end. The mind naturally encourages us to consider the notion that God must also be involved at the cellular level, the molecular level, the atomic level, the subatomic level, down to the quarks and leptons, and beyond any level that humans will ever be able to conceive of. Here is where logic gets tricky; if God is involved in the world, and there are not two gods, one for good and one for bad, then how can we say that God is not just as immanent in what the human mind perceives as negative. Logically, God must also be immanent in the decay of every flower, in every natural disaster, and in every death.

Maimonides proposed that there is an interdependent relationship between the Creator, the creating, and the creation, and that such an interdependence could not be explained through ordinary philosophical analysis. In the seventeenth century, philosopher Baruch Spinoza ran with this idea when he proposed that there is no separation at all between the divine and the natural world. [137] A handful of contemporary religious scholars, including Houston Smith, Paul Tillich, Marcus Borg, and Zalman Schachter-Shalomi, have suggested that the next step to consider in religious thought transcending monotheism might be monism—the notion that there is no separation between the Creator and the creation. In other words, God is the immanent force in all the macro and micro levels of creation imaginable, and the appearance of a separation between Creator and creation is something of an illusion.

The most radical interpretation of God's immanence is taught in Jewish mystical circles where the words of Deuteronomy 4:35 are taken literally. The NRSV renders it: "To you it was shown so that you would acknowledge that the LORD is God; there is no other besides him." This is usually understood to mean that there are no other gods "besides" God. But the Hebrew can be interpreted to mean "there is nothing else besides God." In other words, everything is in God, and God is in everything—nothing is outside of God. Not death, not suffering, not evil, not the greatest star or the smallest particle—it is all part of the Oneness. Unlike pantheism that posits that everything is God, this mystical view of God's imminence is best termed as panentheism: God is in everything. This same idea is found in Christian, Islamic, and Hindu mystical sects. Even this view, however, as enticing as it may be, does not address the questions raised by victims of evil. Try to tell a survivor of rape or genocide that "everything is God" or that "there really is no evil." There is a kind of cruelty and insensitivity in this response if it is our only answer to malevolence.

Ultimately, some rabbis have tried to uncover a godly purpose even in evil. What makes us human is our ability to continually choose good over evil, to make moral decisions even when tempted by immoral forces, and to recognize that within each of us there is always the potential to be good or bad. The rabbis realize, of course, that people are constantly making wrong and immoral choices, but they also recognize that when a person sins and then repents he or she has the chance of being even wiser than before the sin was committed. In other words, through the process of *teshuvah*, "repentance," something good can come out of something bad. Take a look at this magnificent teaching from the Midrash that ascribes honor to darkness through an analogy: "Rabbi Berekhiah said, 'Consider the eyeball. It is not through the white of it that one sees, but through the black'" (Leviticus Rabbah 31:8).

Most religions use the metaphor of light as something good (i.e., enlightenment, and describing an intelligent person as bright) and darkness as akin to blindness. Biologically, it may be that nighttime is felt to be a time of danger. So, the metaphor of light and dark takes on the connotation of good and bad. But just as the dark of the eyeball makes it possible for us to see in the daytime, the analogy can be extended to what we can see in the nighttime sky. During the day, we can't see the stars because light obscures them. But at night—the darker the night the better—we can see a hundred light years away; we can see so far that we are actually seeing back in time.

Contemporary scholar and author Rabbi David Wolpe reminds us that there is so much light in the desert that it's under the shrubs where small animals can be found hiding under the protection of the shade. As one young woman sang to her beloved, "With great delight I sat in his shadow, and his fruit was sweet to my taste" (Song of Solomon 2:3). On the first day of creation God declared that both day and night—morning and evening—are declared to be good. Job confirms this in one of his descriptions of God: "He uncovers the deeps out of darkness, and brings deep darkness to light" (Job 12:22). Finally, the eighteenth-century mystic Rebbe Nachman of Breslov taught from the Zohar that darkness is the cloak of light as much as the body is the cloak of the soul.

We want to say that we worship a loving God, and that is partially true. But God, a God of righteous judgment, also permits hatred to exist in the world. The psalmist says, "The LORD loves those who hate evil" (Ps. 97:10), and we are told there is "a time to love, and a time to hate" (Eccles. 3:8). King Solomon reminds us that "there are six things that the LORD hates, seven that are an abomination to him: haughty eyes, a lying tongue, and hands that shed innocent blood, a heart that devises wicked plans, feet that hurry to run to evil, a lying witness who testifies falsely, and one who sows discord in a family" (Prov. 6:16–19).

5. A Conclusion of Sorts

The greatest theologians and philosophers have never been able to fully resolve the question of why God permits bad things to happen to good people. Our brains seem to be hardwired to want black and white answers, and from this hardwiring come dualistic theologies. As we struggle to understand why evil, natural disasters, and the suffering of the innocent are permitted to exist, God's explanation to Isaiah, "my thoughts are not your thoughts, neither are your ways my ways," is honest and humbling. We really don't know, so we lean on our faith. It's certainly true that when the innocent suffer, we are given the opportunity to show compassion. We are stirred to make it a better world. No single explanation for suffering can be, or should be, satisfying. Our discomfort is the force that impels us forward: to heal the planet, to make the world better in some little way.

Most theologians reluctantly agree to what Isaiah reported—that God indeed does permit evil and suffering to exist, and expects humanity to transform the negative into something good. This is the underlying message of the Exodus in Judaism and of the Resurrection in Christianity. It is this very paradox of good and evil, love and hatred, light and dark, that impels each person to grow and to help in the face of illness, cruelty, and needless suffering. Regarding natural disasters and the suffering of the innocent, we have only the notions of mystery, vicarious atonement, and our faith to fall back on. Every time we hear of an innocent victim's suffering, the Christian is impelled to think of Jesus suffering alongside that victim and the Jew to think of God and the angels weeping alongside every victim.

Rabbi Aron Moss sums it up well when he says that in the end we do not really want or need answers. The Jewish view of covenant is that regardless of who or what causes suffering, our part of the contract with God is to relieve suffering. Regardless of who or what causes disease, our covenantal obligation is to end disease. In the end, the issue of God and evil is purely academic, but the job description of our human covenant with God is clear. Rabbi Moss writes:

> So keep asking the question, "Why do bad things happen to good people?" But stop looking for answers. Start formulating a response. Take your righteous anger and turn it into a force for doing good. Redirect your frustration with injustice and unfairness and channel it into a drive to fight injustice and unfairness. Let your outrage propel you into action. When you see innocent people suffering, help them. Combat the

pain in the world with goodness. Alleviate suffering wherever you can. We don't want answers, we don't want explanations, and we don't want closure. We want an end to suffering. And we dare not leave it up to God to alleviate suffering. He is waiting for us to do it. That's what we are here for.[138]

God's Anthropology of Humanity

A mistake all three Abrahamic religions make is to think the stories in the Scriptures enable the faithful to understand God. Not so. These stories enable the faithful to understand what God wants of us, not how to get what we want from God. Rabbi Abraham Joshua Heschel reminded us that that "the Bible is not primarily man's vision of God, but God's vision of man. The Bible is not man's theology but God's anthropology, dealing with man and what He asks of him rather than the nature of God."[139]

Rabbi Shai Held uncovered a parallel view of the Bible in the writings of Protestant theologian Karl Barth, who wrote, "It is not the right human thoughts about God which form the content of the Bible, but the right divine thoughts about men."[140] Support for Heschel's and Barth's views can be found in both the Elder and Younger Testaments when we read about Job. Job wants to understand the mysterious nature of God and is answered out of the whirlwind:

> "Who is this that darkens counsel by words without knowledge? Gird up your loins like a man, I will question you, and you shall declare to me. Where were you when I laid the foundation of the earth? Tell me, if you have understanding." (Job 38:2–4)

Paul, in like manner, seeks to correct the errors of the Corinthian community when he asks, "For what human being knows what is truly human except the human spirit that is within? So also no one comprehends what is truly God's except the Spirit of God" (1 Cor. 2:11). While Jews, Christians, and Muslims don't have perfect theology—knowledge of God—we can rest assured that God has a perfect anthropology of humanity. Scripture offers us a clear understanding of our obligations in what both Rabbi Akiva and Rabbi Jesus said was among the greatest of the commandments: to love your neighbor as yourself.

Books

Barmash, Pamela, and W. David Nelson, eds. *Exodus in the Jewish Experience: Echoes and Reverberations*. Lanham, MD: Lexington Books, 2015.

Biale, David. *Cultures of the Jews*. Vol. 1, *Mediterranean Origins*. New York: Schocken Books, 2002.

Brenner, Athalya, and Gail A. Yee, eds. *Exodus and Deuteronomy*. Minneapolis: Fortress Press, 2012.

Brodt, Sholom. *Exodus: The Model of Personal Liberation*. Jerusalem: Yeshivat Simchat Shlomo, 2013.

Chase, Mary Ellen. *Life and Language in the Old Testament*. New York: W. W. Norton, 1955.

Chelst, Kenneth. *Exodus and Emancipation—Biblical and African-American Slavery*. Brooklyn, NY: Urim Publications, 2009.

Coffey, John. *Exodus and Liberation—Deliverance Politics from John Calvin to Martin Luther King Jr*. Oxford: Oxford University Press, 2014.

Dosick, Wayne. *The Real Name of God: Embracing the Full Essence of the Divine*. Rochester, VT: Inner Traditions, 2012.

Eban, Abba. *Heritage Civilization and the Jews*. New York: Summit Books, 1984.

Edinger, Edward F. *The Bible and the Psyche—Individuation Symbolism in the Old Testament*. Toronto, ON: Inner City Books, 1986.

Frymer-Kensky, Tikva, and David Novak, Michael A. Signer, David Fox Sandmel, and Peter Ochs, eds. *Christianity in Jewish Terms*. Boulder, CO: Westview Press, 2000.

Gottheimer, Josh. *Ripples of Hope: Great American Civil Rights Speeches*. New York: Civitas Books, 2003.

Greenberg, Irving. *The Jewish Way: Living the Holidays*. New York: Touchstone, 1988.

Halevi, Z'ev ben Shimon. *Kabbalah and Exodus*. York Beach, ME: Samuel Weiser Inc., 1988.

Harris, Maurice D. *Moses, A Stranger among Us*. Eugene, OR: Cascade Books, 2012.

Houck, Davis W., and David E. Dixon, eds. *Rhetoric, Religion and the Civil Rights Movement*. Waco, TX: Baylor University Press, 2006.

Kamenetz, Rodger. *The Jew in the Lotus*. San Francisco: HarperSanFrancisco, 1994.

————. *Stalking Elijah—Adventures with Today's Jewish Mystical Masters*. San Francisco: HarperSanFrancisco, 1997.

Kluger, Rivkah Scharf. *Psyche in Scripture—The Idea of the Chosen People and Other Essays*. Toronto: Inner City Books, 1995.

Kook, Abraham Isaac. *The Lights of Penitence*. Translated by Ben Zion Bokser. Mahwah, NJ: Paulist Press, 1978.

Kushner, Lawrence. *The River of Light: Spirituality, Judaism, Consciousness*. Woodstock, VT: Jewish Lights Publishing, 1990.

Langston, Scott M. *Exodus Through the Centuries*. Hoboken, NJ: Blackwell Publishing Ltd., 2006.

Levine, Amy-Jill. *The Misunderstood Jew*. San Francisco: HarperCollins, 2006.

Matt, Daniel. *Zohar: The Book of Enlightenment*. New York: Paulist Press, 1983.

Prager, Dennis, and Joseph Telushkin. *Why the Jews: The Reasons for Anti-Semitism*. New York: Touchstone Books, 1983.

Raboteau, Albert J. *Slave Religion: The Invisible Institution in the Antebellum South*. Oxford: Oxford University Press, 2004.

Rollins, Wayne G. *Soul and Psyche: The Bible in Psychological Perspective*. Minneapolis: Fortress Press, 1999.

Rosenthal, Robert. *Plagues to Miracles*. Carlsbad, CA: Hay House, 2012.

Sarna, Nahum M. *Exploring Exodus—The Heritage of Biblical Israel*. New York: Schocken, 1986.

Sasso, Sandy Eisenberg. *Midrash: Reading the Bible with Question Marks*. Brewster, MA: Paraclete Press, 2013.

Schachter-Shalomi, Zalman. *Jewish with Feeling*. New York: Riverhead Books, 2005.

Scholer, David M., ed. *The Works of Philo*. Translated by Charles Duke Younge. Peabody, MA: Hendrickson, 1993.

Selby, Gary S. *Martin Luther King and the Rhetoric of Freedom*. Waco, TX: Baylor University Press, 2008.

Spiegel, Shalom. *The Last Trial—The Akedah*. Woodstock, VT: Jewish Lights Publishing, 1993.

Walker, David. *Walker's Appeal, In Four Articles*. Chapel Hill: University of North Carolina Press, 2011.

Walzer, Michael. *Exodus and Revolution*. New York: Basic Books, Inc., 1985.

Washington, James M., ed. *A Testament of Hope: The Essential Writings of Martin Luther King, Jr.* New York: Harper & Row, 1986.

Waskow, Arthur. *Seasons of Our Joy*. Boston: Beacon, 1982.

Zaslow, David, and Joseph Lieberman. *Jesus: First-Century Rabbi*. Brewster, MA: Paraclete Press, 2013.

———. *Thou Shalt Wander Forty Years: Selected Poetry and Artwork*. Ashland, OR: The Wisdom Exchange, 2006.

Torah with Commentaries

Hertz, J. H. *Pentateuch & Haftorahs*. London: Soncino Press, 1936.

Hirsch, Samson Raphael. *The Pentateuch*. 7 vols. London, England: Gateshead: Judaica Press, 1989.

Munk, Ellie, ed. *The Call of the Torah*. 5 vols. Brooklyn, NY: Mesorah, 1995.

Plaut, W. Gunther, ed. *The Torah*. New York: UAHC Press, 1981.

Scherman, Nosson, ed. *The Chumash: The Stone Edition*. Brooklyn, NY: Mesorah, 1993.

Collections of Midrash

Bialik, Hayim Nahman, and Yohoshua Hana Ravnitzky, eds. *The Book of Legends*. New York: Schocken Books, 1992.

Ginzberg, Louis. *Legends of the Jews*. 2 vols. Philadelphia: Jewish Publication Society, 2003.

Hammer, Reuven. *The Classic Midrash*. Mahwah, NJ: Paulist Press, 1995.

Scherman, Nosson, ed. *Kleinman Edition Midrash Rabbah*. 17 vols. Brooklyn, NY: Mesorah, 2011.

Weissman, Moshe, ed. *The Midrash Says*. 5 vols. Brooklyn, NY: Benei Yakov Publications, 1982.

Haggadah with Commentary

Kagan, Michael L. *The Holistic Haggadah*. Jerusalem: Urim Publications, 2004.

Mykoff, Moshe. *The Breslov Haggadah*. Jerusalem: Breslov Research Institute, 1989.

Sender, Yitzchak. *The Commentators' Haggadah*. Spring Valley, New York: Feldheim, 1991.

Touger, Eliyahu, trans. and ed. *The Chasidic Haggahdah*. New York: Moznaim, 1998.

NOTES

1   See the excellent book by Rabbi Sandy Eisenberg Sasso called *Midrash: Reading the Bible with Question Marks* (Brewster, MA: Paraclete Press, 2013).

2   Full review at http://www.patheos.com/blogs/takeandread/2013/12jesus-first-century-rabbi-a-tale-of-love-and-caution/.

3   A proof text in Judaism and Christianity is when a person supports a theological idea by quoting an often brief text in the Bible to "prove" its veracity.

4   E. W. Bullinger, *Figures of Speech Used in the Bible* (Grand Rapids, MI: Baker Publishing, 1968), vi–vii.

5   Mary Ellen Chase, *Life and Language in the Old Testament* (New York: W. W. Norton, 1955), 119.

6   From *A Thought for the Week*, adapted from the works of Menachem M. Schneerson by Y. M. Kagan, p. 43. Based on Likuttei Sichos, vol. 2, p. 348 (Brooklyn, NY: Merkos Publishing, 1983).

7   The emigration of large numbers of African Americans leaving the South after the Civil War took approximately four or five decades.

8   Irving Greenberg, *The Jewish Way: Living the Holidays* (New York: Touchstone, 1988), 25.

9   Krista Tippett, *On Being, Krista's Journal: The Necessity of Desire for Liberation* (blog), March 29, 2007, http://www.onbeing.org/program/exodus-cargo-hidden-stories/journal/2384.

10 Abigail E. Gillman, "From Myth to Memory," in *Exodus in the Jewish Experience* (Lanham, MD: Lexington Books, 2015), 194.

11 Lawrence Kushner, *The River of Light: Spirituality, Judaism, Consciousness* (Woodstock, VT: Jewish Lights Publishing, 1990), 124.

12 David Brion Davis, "Exiles, Exodus and Promised Lands," Tanner Lectures on Human Values (New Haven, CT: Yale University Press, 2006), 127.

13 Scott M. Langston, *Exodus Through the Centuries* (Hoboken, NJ: Blackwell Publishing Ltd., 2006), 3.

14 Ibid.

15 John Coffey, *Exodus and Liberation—Deliverance Politics from John Calvin to Martin Luther King Jr.* (New York City: Oxford University Press, 2014), 4–5.

16 Abraham Joshua Heschel, "Toward an Understanding of Halachah," *Conservative Judaism and Jewish Law* (1977): 134.

17 Pamela Barmash, *Exodus in the Jewish Experience: Echoes and Reverberations*, eds. Pamela Barmash and W. David Nelson (Lanham, MD: Lexington Books, 2015), vii.

18 David Biale, *Cultures of the Jews*, vol. 1, *Mediterranean Origins* (New York: Schocken Books, 2002), 17.

19 Gillman, *Exodus in the Jewish Experience*, 207.

20   Scott M. Langston, *Exodus Through the Centuries*, 114.

21   Samson Raphael Hirsch, *The Pentateuch*, vol. 2 (Gateshead, London, UK: Judaica Press, 1989), 135.

22   Gillman, *Exodus in the Jewish Experience*, 195.

23   Robert Rosenthal, *Plagues to Miracles* (Carlsbad, CA: Hay House, 2012), 239.

24   Greenberg, *The Jewish Way*, 25.

25   Zalman Schachter-Shalomi, *Age-ing to Sage-ing* (New York: Warner Books, 1995), 33–35 citing Gerald Heard, *The Five Ages of Man* (New York: Julian Press, 1964).

26   See also the timeline by Elizer Shulman in *The Sequence of Events in the Old Testament* (Tel Aviv, Israel: Investment Co. of Bank Hapoalim and Ministry of Defense Publishing House, 1987), 79. Rabbi Aryeh Kaplan's comment about the Hebrews residing in *Ritmah* or *Kadesh* for nineteen years is from *The Living Torah* (New York: Maznaim Publishing), 845.

27   J. H. Hertz, *The Pentateuch and Haftorahs* (London: Soncino Press, 1936), 714.

28   From http://www.sichosinenglish.org/books/in-the-garden-of-the-torah/42.htm. June 1, 2016.

29   From http://njjewishnews.com/njjn.com/073108/porCorrectingCourse.html. June 1, 2016.

30   Biblical Hebrew lexicons are available on several websites (e.g., https://www.blueletterbible.org/), where etymological word studies can be found for the names of all forty-two campsites on the Exodus listed in Numbers 33:5–49.

31   Mary Ellen Chase, *Life and Language in the Old Testament* (New York: W. W. Norton, 1955), 125–27.

32   See http://www.myjewishlearning.com/article/lost-stories/. June 1, 2016.

33   Batya may be the same "daughter of Pharaoh" who is called Bithiah in 1 Chronicles 4:17.

34   Edward F. Edinger, *The Bible and the Psyche—Individuation Symbolism in the Old Testament* (Toronto, ON: Inner City Books, 1986), 47.

35   David Gelernter, *Psychological Criticism of Biblical Narrative*, Hebraic Political Studies, vol. 4, no. 3 (Summer 2009): 225. Gelernter was a senior fellow in Jewish thought at the Shalem Center in Jerusalem.

36   See http://gnosis.org/naghamm/gthlamb.html, saying #82. June 1, 2016.

37   David Slabotsky, *The Mind of Genesis* (Ottawa, ON: Valley Editions, 1975).

38   Zalman Schachter-Shalomi, *Jewish with Feeling* (New York: Riverhead Books, 2005), 27.

39   Midrash Rabbah, Exodus 3:6 as cited by Peter Ochs, "The God of Jews and Christians" in *Christianity in Jewish Terms*, ed. Tikva Frymer-Kensky, David Novak, Michael A. Signer, David Fox Sandmel, and Peter Ochs (Boulder, CO: Westview Press, 2000), 55.

40   See http://www.myjewishlearning.com/article/hardened-hearts-some-explanations/. June 1, 2016.

41 Hertz, *The Pentateuch and Haftorahs*, 220.

42 Jewish religious consultants for the animation were Dr. Burton Visotsky, Dr. Evertt Fox, Rabbi Stephen Robbins, and Rabbi Shoshanna Gershenzon.

43 Maurice D. Harris, *Moses, A Stranger among Us* (Eugene, OR: Cascade Books, 2012), 22–23.

44 Gary S. Selby, *Martin Luther King and the Rhetoric of Freedom* (Waco, TX: Baylor University Press, 2008), 63.

45 See http://www.dalailama.com/news/post/949-conference-on-resilience-strength -through-compassion-and-connection-in-new-orleans. June 1, 2016.

46 Rabbi Ronald Isaacs, *Derech Eretz* (New York: National Youth Commission, United Synagogue of Conservative Judaism, 1995), 38. From Avot de-Rabbi Natan, 23.

47 Other passages include Exodus 9:16; Exodus 9:27–28; Exodus 11:3; Exodus 14:4; Exodus 14:18; Isaiah 19:21.

48 Zarum, http://www.thejc.com/judaism/judaism-features/117467/why-did-we-sing -when-egyptians-drowned.

49 Philo, *The Works of Philo*, trans. Charles Duke Younge, ed. David M. Scholer (Peabody, MA: Hendrickson, 1993), 406.

50 Ibid., 468.

51 Langston, *Exodus Through the Centuries*, 91–92.

52 Ibid., 92.

53 Rosenthal, *Plagues to Miracles*, 89.

54 *Likkutei Sichot*, vol. 2, Shemot (Brooklyn, NY: Kehot Publishing, 1983), 23–25.

55 Ibid.

56 Edinger, *The Bible and the Psyche*, 49–51.

57 See http://www.come-and-hear.com/sotah/sotah_37.html. June 1, 2016.

58 Talmud, Megillah 10b and Sanhedrin 39b.

59 Raphael Zarum, http://www.thejc.com/judaism/judaism-features/117467/why-did -we-sing-when-egyptians-drowned. June 1, 2016.

60 Kushner, *The River of Light*, 124.

61 Jerusalem Talmud: Nedarim 9:4.

62 See http://www.myjewishlearning.com/article/the-shavuot-marriage-contract/2/ or an abridged version by Howard Schwartz, *Reimagining the Bible: The Storytelling of the Rabbis* (New York: Oxford University Press, 1998), 87.

63 Mary Baker G. Eddy, *Science & Health* (Boston, MA: Christian Science Publishing Society, 1875), 566.

64 Lawrence Kushner, *Honey from the Rock* (Woodstock, VT: Jewish Lights Publishing, 2000), 22.

65 Harris, *Moses, A Stranger among Us*, xvii–xviii.

66 Greenberg, *The Jewish Way*, 65.

67 Talmud, Pesakhim 116b.

68 From the essay "Christian Worship" by Robert Louis Wilken in *Christianity in Jewish Terms*, 200.

69 Ibid., 184.

70 Barmash, *Exodus in the Jewish Experience*, viii–ix.

71 Michael Walzer, *Exodus and Revolution* (New York: Basic Books, Inc., 1985), 12.

72 W.G. Plaut, trans. and ed., *The Torah* (New York: Union of American Hebrew Congregations, 1981), 1,240.

73 Wilken, *Christianity in Jewish Terms*, 200.

74 Available at http://www.nobelprize.org/nobel_prizes/peace/laureates/1986 /wiesel-lecture.html.

75 Kalman P. Bland, "Passover and Thanatos in Medieval Jewish Consciousness," in *Exodus in the Jewish Experience*, 148.

76 Creative Commons Copyright © 1992 by Arthur Waskow. Attribution: NoDerivs CC BY-ND. See https://theshalomcenter.org/node/229, and Arthur Waskow, *Godwrestling—Round 2: Ancient Wisdom, Future Paths* (Nashville, TN: Jewish Lights, 1996), 328–29.

77 Martin Buber, *Ten Rungs* (New York: Schocken Books, 1947), 54.

78 David Zaslow and Joseph Lieberman, *Jesus: First-Century Rabbi* (Brewster, MA: Paraclete Press, 2014).

79 Dr. Louis E. Newman, *The Meaning and Practice of Teshuvah* (Woodstock, VT: Jewish Lights Publishing, 2010), 198.

80 See http://juchre.org/talmud/sanhedrin/sanhedrin6.htm.

81 Clark Williamson, "A Christian View of Redemption," in *Christianity in Jewish Terms*, 287–88.

82 Abraham Isaac Kook, *The Lights of Penitence*, trans. Ben Zion Bokser (Mahwah, NJ: Paulist Press, 1978), 85.

83 John J. Collins, *Apocalypse, Prophesy, and Pseudepigraphy* (Grand Rapids, MI: Wm. B. Eerdmans Publishing Co., 2015), 140.

84 Leora Batnitzky, "On the Suffering of God's Chosen," in *Christianity in Jewish Terms*, 218.

85 Talmud: Sotah 14a, http://www.come-and-hear.com/sotah/sotah_14.html.

86 Batnitzky, *Christianity in Jewish Terms*, 206.

87 Irving Greenberg, "Confronting the Holocaust Again," in *For the Sake of Heaven and Earth* (Philadelphia: Jewish Publication Society, 2004), 25.

88 Thomas Merton, *Conjectures of a Guilty Bystander* (Garden City, NY: Doubleday, 1966).

89 Robert Gibbs, "Suspicions of Suffering," *Christianity in Jewish Terms*, 226.

90 Batnitzky, 214 citing Hermann Cohen, *Religion of Reason Out of the Sources of Judaism* (New York: Frederick Unger Publishing, 1971), 268.

91 Cheryl A. Kirk-Duggan, "How Liberating Is the Exodus and for Whom?" in *Exodus and Deuteronomy*, ed. Athalya Brenner and Gail A. Yee (Minneapolis:

Fortress Press, 2012), 15.

92 Coffey, *Exodus and Liberation*, 14.

93 Langston, *Exodus Through the Centuries*, 5–7.

94 The Koran also retells the Exodus story with the benefit of Talmudic interpretations and New Testament references. Islamic scholarship also has much to bring to the table of interfaith dialogue.

95 Langston, *Exodus Through the Centuries*, 113.

96 Ibid., 112–13.

97 Ibid., 112.

98 Robert Scribner, "Incombustible Luther," *Past and Present* 110 (1968): 47–48.

99 Coffey, *Exodus and Liberation*, 31.

100 Ibid., 38.

101 Elizabeth Suer, "The Peculiar Status of Early Modern England," in *Reading the Nation*, ed. Elizabeth Suer and Julia M. Wright (London: Routledge, 2009), 146.

102 Coffey, *Exodus and Liberation*, 25–26.

103 Wayne G. Rollins, *Soul and Psyche: The Bible in Psychological Perspective* (Minneapolis: Fortress Press, 1999), 176.

104 Coffey, *Exodus and Liberation*, 97.

105 Lance J. Sussman, "Exodus as a Theme in American History and Culture," http://projudaism.org/wp-content/uploads/2015/04/Passover-Message.pdf. June 1, 2016.

106 See http://www.jubilee-centre.org/the-abolition-of-the-slave-trade-christian-conscience-and-political-action-by-john-coffey/. June 1, 2016.

107 Kirk-Duggan, *Exodus and Deuteronomy*, 25.

108 Heschel's talk was called "The Religious Basis for Equality and Opportunity" at the National Catholic Conference for Interracial Justice held on January 14, 1963.

109 Davis W. Houck and David E. Dixon, eds., *Rhetoric, Religion and the Civil Rights Movement* (Waco, TX: Baylor University Press, 2006), 733.

110 Ibid., 903–4.

111 Josh Gottheimer, *Ripples of Hope: Great American Civil Rights Speeches* (New York: Civitas Books, 2003), 46.

112 See http://www.harriettubman.com/callhermoses.html. June 1, 2016.

113 James M. Washington, ed., *A Testament of Hope: The Essential Writings of Martin Luther King, Jr.* (New York: Harper & Row, 1986), 279–86.

114 Selby, *Martin Luther King and the Rhetoric of Freedom*, 9–10.

115 Coffey, *Exodus and Liberation*, 216.

116 Ibid., 8–9.

117 Amy-Jill Levine, *The Misunderstood Jew* (San Francisco: HarperCollins, 2006), 8.

118 Mark Galli, "A Fully Biblical Liberation," *Christianity Today* (October 14, 2011), 50.

119 From *A Report on the Puebla Meeting of the Latin American Bishops' Conference* in ADL Memorandum (New York: Anti-Defamation League, March 14, 1979), 7. The full article is at http://americanjewisharchives.org/publications/journal /PDF/1983_35_01_00_klenicki.pdf.

120 Greenberg, *The Jewish Way*, 39.

121 Richard S. Sarason, "The Past as Paradigm," in *Exodus in the Jewish Experience*, 81.

122 The seder was held on April 4, 1969, in a black church in Washington, DC, on behalf of the civil rights movement. Surviving footage of the Freedom Seder can be viewed at https://www.youtube.com/watch?v=U5HgiGMqh6g#t=308.

123 Langston, *Exodus Through the Centuries*, 7.

124 Coffey, *Exodus and Liberation*, 215.

125 Rodger Kamenetz, *The Jew in the Lotus* (San Francisco: HarperSanFrancisco, 1994), 30.

126 Rodger Kamenetz, *Stalking Elijah: Adventures with Today's Jewish Mystical Masters* (San Francisco: HarperSanFrancisco, 1997), 289.

127 Ibid., 288.

128 Ibid., 309.

129 Ibid., 318.

130 From a broadsheet entitled *A Message from His Holiness the Dalai Lama* distributed to synagogues for use in community seders, International Campaign for Tibet, March 5, 1997, http://www.huffingtonpost.com/ellen-frankel/the-power-of -passover-for-jews-and-buddhists_b_2863043.html.

131 Philo, *The Works of Philo*, 342.

132 See Genesis 29:32—35:18.

133 See Genesis 22:14; Genesis 28:19; Genesis 32:2; Genesis 32:30; Exodus 17:7; Numbers 11:3; Numbers 13:24; Joshua 5:9; Joshua 7:26; and Judges 2:5.

134 From the title of Harold Kushner's best-selling book *Why Bad Things Happen to Good People* (New York: Harper Collins, 1981).

135 Byron L. Sherman, *Faith Finding Meaning: A Theology of Judaism* (New York: Oxford University Press, 2009), 130.

136 Mishneh Torah, Teshuva 5:5. Maimonides lived in the thirteenth century and was the head of the Jewish community in Egypt.

137 In 1656, the leadership of the Portuguese Jewish Community of Amsterdam excommunicated Spinoza for his radical philosophy rooted in monistic rationalism.

138 See http://www.chabad.org/library/article_cdo/aid/622117/jewish/Why-Do-Bad -Things-Happen-to-Good-People.htm. June 1, 2016.

139 Abraham Joshua Heschel, *Man Is Not Alone: A Philosophy of Religion* (New York: Farrar, Straus, and Giroux, 1951), 129.

140 Karl Barth, *The Word of God and the Word of Man* (Gloucester, MA: Peter Smith Publisher, 1978), 207–8.

Who We Are

Paraclete Press is a publisher of books, recordings, and DVDs on Christian spirituality. Our publishing represents a full expression of Christian belief and practice—from Catholic to Evangelical, from Protestant to Orthodox.

We are the publishing arm of the Community of Jesus, an ecumenical monastic community in the Benedictine tradition. As such, we are uniquely positioned in the marketplace without connection to a large corporation and with informal relationships to many branches and denominations of faith.

What We Are Doing

PARACLETE PRESS BOOKS | Paraclete publishes books that show the richness and depth of what it means to be Christian. Although Benedictine spirituality is at the heart of who we are and all that we do, we publish books that reflect the Christian experience across many cultures, time periods, and houses of worship. We publish books that nourish the vibrant life of the church and its people.

We have several different series, including the best-selling Paraclete Essentials and Paraclete Giants series of classic texts in contemporary English; Voices from the Monastery— men and women monastics writing about living a spiritual life today; our award-winning Paraclete Poetry series as well as the Mount Tabor Books on the arts; best-selling gift books for children on the occasions of baptism and first communion; and the Active Prayer Series that brings creativity and liveliness to any life of prayer.

MOUNT TABOR BOOKS | Paraclete's newest series, Mount Tabor Books, focuses on the arts and literature as well as liturgical worship and spirituality, and was created in conjunction with the Mount Tabor Ecumenical Centre for Art and Spirituality in Barga, Italy.

PARACLETE RECORDINGS | From Gregorian chant to contemporary American choral works, our recordings celebrate the best of sacred choral music composed through the centuries that create a space for heaven and earth to intersect. Paraclete Recordings is the record label representing the internationally acclaimed choir Gloriæ Dei Cantores, praised for their rapt and fathomless spiritual intensity by *American Record Guide*; the Gloriæ Dei Cantores Schola, specializing in the study and performance of Gregorian chant; and the other instrumental artists of the Arts Empowering Life Foundation.

Paraclete Press is also privileged to be the exclusive North American distributor of the recordings of the Monastic Choir of St. Peter's Abbey in Solesmes, France, long considered to be a leading authority on Gregorian chant.

PARACLETE VIDEO | Our DVDs offer spiritual help, healing, and biblical guidance for a broad range of life issues including grief and loss, marriage, forgiveness, facing death, bullying, addictions, Alzheimer's, and spiritual formation.

Learn more about us at our website
www.paracletepress.com or phone us toll-free at 1.800.451.5006

SCAN
TO
READ
MORE

You may also be interested in . . .

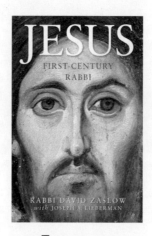

Jesus
First-Century Rabbi
Rabbi David Zaslow with Joseph A. Lieberman

$16.99 | ISBN 978-1-61261-644-5 | Paperback

This bold, fresh look at the historical Jesus and the Jewish roots of Christianity challenges both Jews and Christians to re-examine their understanding of Jesus's commitment to his Jewish faith. Instead of emphasizing the differences between the two religions, this groundbreaking book explains how the concepts of vicarious atonement, mediation, incarnation, and Trinity are actually rooted in classical Judaism.

"This an important book, for Christians and Jews alike. Rabbi Zaslow has tried to stimulate a conversation and build bridges between the two faiths. This is a critically important task, and this book makes that attempt with broad scholarship and great clarity."
—REV. JOHN M. SALMON, PhD, Princeton Theological Seminary

Available through your local bookseller or through Paraclete Press:
www.paracletepress.com; 1-800-451-5006